Images of Modern America

LGBT SALT LAKE

For the seventh year in a row, the LGBT community worked to pass a nondiscrimination bill that would have added sexual orientation and gender identity as a protected class from employment and housing discrimination. The LGBT community rallied at the state capitol in 2014 to show support for Sen. Steve Urquhart's (R-St. George) bill, which the legislature refused to hear. (Courtesy David Daniels.)

FRONT COVER: Beginning in the 1970s, members of the gay and lesbian community began to gather in parks as part of Gay Pride Day, but in 1990, they took to the streets to march for the first time. From this modest beginning, when only several dozen lesbian, gay, bisexual, and transgender people marched through the streets of Salt Lake City proclaiming Gay Pride, the Pride celebration has grown to become the second-largest parade and festival in Utah, attracting thousands of people each June. (Courtesy David Daniels.)

UPPER BACK COVER: Members of Queer Nation march from the capitol building through the streets of downtown during the 1992 Gay Pride March in Salt Lake City. (Courtesy Curtis Jensen.)

LOWER BACK COVER: (left) The March on Washington in 1993 brought thousands of LGBT rights advocates from all over the country onto the National Mall. They called for government action on a variety of issues, including employment protections, the right to serve openly in the military, the repeal of sodomy laws, and more funding for HIV/AIDS education and treatment. LGBT rights activists from Utah joined the march. (Courtesy Curtis Jensen.) **(center)** The Bad Kids Collective formed in 2012 as a community of queer artists. They are performance artists who push boundaries on the ideas of drag, gender, and art. Their work resists conformity and helps create safe spaces for people who feel marginalized. (Courtesy Aaron Michael Woods; see page 80.) **(right)** Queer Nation began in New York City in 1990. By February 1991, activists in Utah formed a chapter to promote queer visibility and to fight back against homophobia. Members deployed a language of liberation that harkened back to the days of the Gay Liberation Front. (Courtesy Curtis Jensen.)

Images of Modern America

LGBT SALT LAKE

J. SETH ANDERSON

ISBN 978-1-4671-2585-7

Published by Arcadia Publishing
Charleston, South Carolina

Printed in the United States of America

Library of Congress Control Number: 2017932975

For all general information, please contact Arcadia Publishing:
Telephone 843-853-2070
Fax 843-853-0044
E-mail sales@arcadiapublishing.com
For customer service and orders:
Toll-Free 1-888-313-2665

Visit us on the Internet at www.arcadiapublishing.com

To the new and everlasting queers, for fulfilling the measure of their creation

Contents

ACKNOWLEDGMENTS

I am forever grateful to so many people who have shaped my thinking, helped refine my scholarship, and encouraged me to continue my work. I must give a huge thanks to my graduate school advisor, Dr. Beth Clement, who took me under her wing and taught me how to read, write, and think like a historian. I thank Kathryn Stockton for her friendship and queer ideas and D. Michael Quinn for his research in the 1990s. Ben Williams must be thanked for his foresight in preserving dozens of boxes of primary sources pertaining to the gay and lesbian community in Utah, without which a project like this would be difficult to complete. Thanks go to Connell O'Donovan for his research and ideas and to Doug Winkler for writing such a brilliant dissertation. I thank Brad Westwood at the state archives for having vision. I thank Dr. Kristen Ries and Maggie Snyder for their friendship and their heroic work treating people with AIDS when few others would. Kristen and Maggie deserve all the praise they get and more. Thanks go to all who contributed photographs for this project when I e-mailed out of the blue to ask for them. This includes Beano Solomon, Ben Barr, David Newkirk, Curtis Jensen, Scott Stites, Jolene Mewing, Courtney Moser, the Royal Court of the Golden Spike Empire, Scott McCoy, Becky Moss, Michael Aaron, and Stephen Justesen, to name only a few. I extend a huge thanks to David Daniels for documenting the movement in a post–Prop 8 world and for sharing his work with me. Thanks go to Nikki Boyer and Joe Redburn and to the LGBT community in Salt Lake City, who have supported this project and who turned over photographs and ephemera and shared their stories and experiences. Thanks go to Chris Schaefer and Doug Smith for their financial support. I also thank the staff at the J. Willard Marriott Library Special Collections at the University of Utah and Stacia Bannerman at Arcadia Publishing. Last but not least, I thank my husband, Dr. Michael Ferguson, who changed my life forever.

Introduction

Salt Lake City is a town full of secrets. Some secrets are hidden intentionally, while others are hidden in plain sight. One such secret is the history of the lesbian, gay, bisexual, and transgender communities in the city and the state. Long before culture had the language or concepts to identify sexual orientation and gender identity, people who we would now label as LGBT have called Utah home. Utah and Salt Lake City have a vibrant LGBT community, but the general public knows little about its history. Salt Lake City was not a gay metropolis like New York City or San Francisco, but by the 1970s, it was also not a small, rural town. Rather, the city occupied a space somewhere in the middle of these extremes. For some people, Salt Lake City felt provincial and a place from which they longed to escape. Yet others left their rural Utah towns for Salt Lake City, which they considered a big city in relation to where they had grown up. Brigham Young University also attracted a steady flow of young men and women to Utah County who traveled between Provo and Salt Lake City in search of others who shared their desires for love with a person of the same sex. Enough people moved into Salt Lake City after World War II that a small, urban gay subculture began to emerge. While Gay Liberation and organizations that would fight for the political rights of LGBT citizens were years away from forming, a small number of people in Salt Lake City recognized why they were different, often struggled to reconcile their sexual desires with their religious upbringings, and began to take small steps out of the closet.

By the late 1940s and early 1950s, several bars in town cautiously accepted the city's sexual minorities as customers. The Radio City Lounge opened at 147 South State Street in 1948 and within a decade became known as a bar where gay and lesbian people could meet in a relatively safe public space hidden beneath the heterosexual clientele. By the early 1950s, gays and lesbians began frequenting the Crystal Lounge at 174 South State Street. However, by 1957, the owners no longer welcomed gay and lesbian customers, because fear of exposure to law enforcement threatened the business. By the 1960s, the Tin Angel at 340 South State Street hosted female impersonation shows that drew a large crowd of straight-identified customers, which threatened to give away the secret (and safety) of gays and lesbians in Salt Lake City.

This book has two main purposes. The first aims to celebrate the history and people of Utah who worked for decades to establish a safer, kinder, and more just world for citizens who do not identify as heterosexual. Many of these efforts, from publishing the first gay and lesbian newsletters to confronting the devastating effects of AIDS and protecting the rights of LGBT youth, are heroic and must never be forgotten. The second purpose aims to shine a light on the historicity of what we now call the "LGBT community" in Utah. Unlike other sciences, the study of history is not esoteric. I do not believe professional historians have tried to obfuscate their work with confusing concepts or jargon in an effort to exclude everyone except other professionals from the study of sexuality in history. But the question becomes, how can one tune into the multiplicity of voices that have revealed in great depth the history of sexuality? How can one come to terms with the components of queer theory as well as issues of class, race, and gender analysis that shapes this field of study? How can one understand the debates and feel the excitement that comes from the creation of knowledge? I hope this book provides a helpful road map to people who may be unfamiliar with the history of sexuality but who are curious to learn how the LGBT community in Salt Lake City formed, how it defined itself, and the struggles and successes this movement has had over the decades.

A challenge when writing about identities and sexual categories is that they are not eternal. Gender and sexual orientation are socially constructed categories with historical antecedents that function in particular ways depending on time and place. These categories are unstable, are always under negotiation and renegotiation, and have been deployed at different times for different reasons. Writing historically about gender and sexual orientation presents difficulty, because the historian must be vigilant to not impose current understandings of these categories onto people of the past. As historian George Chauncey observes in his book *Gay New York*, doing so obscures more than it illuminates. For example, after 1969, the movement for Gay Liberation encompassed all sexual minorities, since people accepted the word *gay* as a capacious term. By the mid-1970s, the word *lesbian* began to mark an important distinction between men and women. By the late 1980s, gays and lesbians began using the word *queer* as a way to define themselves, reappropriating a word that had long been an ugly slur. By the 1990s, use of *LGBT* came into mainstream parlance and as of this writing continues to expand with new letters and even numbers. Such impermanence makes writing about these identities a challenge. I differentiate the terms *gay* and *lesbian* and *LGBT* accordingly.

Chapter 1 traces the history of Utah from the 19th century to 1969. I use the term *queer* in this chapter to mean peculiar. People we would now call lesbian, gay, bisexual, and transgender lived in Utah during these years, but no community existed at this time. Too much exposure risked arrest and imprisonment in jail or the mental institution. Chapter 2 explores the emergence of this community in Utah when Gay Liberation arrived after 1969. The gay and lesbian community backed defensively into the 1980s, and chapter 3 explores the emergence of AIDS in Utah and the organizations that began to fight the epidemic. Grassroots efforts to raise money for treatment and education resulted in the formation of the Salt Lake AIDS Foundation, AIDS Project Utah, and other support groups. AIDS activists such as David Sharpton, Sheldon Spears, Patty Reagan, and Ben Barr poured their souls into their work in hopes of saving lives, educating the public, and helping people die with dignity. Dr. Kristen Ries and physician assistant Maggie Snyder treated the majority of people with AIDS in Utah for nearly a decade in their private practice before moving to Clinic 1A at the University of Utah Hospital. Chapter 4 explores the growing influence of gays and lesbians politically. By the early 1990s, gays and lesbians in Utah as well as around the country began to have more influence within politics. David Nelson founded the Gay and Lesbian Utah Democrats in 1990. The Democratic Party showed a willingness to include gays and lesbians openly, although that relationship was often strained. The formation of a Gay Straight Alliance at East High School by student Kelli Peterson put Utah at the center of a national debate about gay and lesbian students and their rights at school. In 1998, Jackie Biskupski won a seat in the Utah House of Representatives as an openly gay candidate. By the beginning of the 21st century, opposition to marriage equality intensified, culminating in a flurry of constitutional amendments nationwide. Utah marched in step with this tide of growing antigay rhetoric by passing Amendment 3. A legal challenge to Amendment 3 nearly a decade after its passage would play an important role in moving the country towards national marriage equality.

Chapter 5 focuses on how Proposition 8 in California united the LGBT community in Utah to become even more politically active and alert. Support from the LDS Church for California's Proposition 8, which rescinded marriage rights of LGBT people, incensed the LGBT community nationally. In Utah, LGBT people turned that anger and frustration into a renewed commitment to seek social justice and equality. Chapter 6 marks the turn into a Queer New World. Several LGBT candidates won elections and pushed for more inclusive LGBT rights. In December 2013, after a federal judge struck down Amendment 3, same-sex couples began to marry in Utah. A legal battle ensued for nearly a year before the Supreme Court refused to hear the state's appeal, thus returning legal same-sex marriage to Utah. After such a historic win, the LGBT community has had to prioritize other important issues, such as securing rights for transgender people, passing hate crime legislation, fighting to end conversion therapy, and supporting LGBT youth.

This book is a photographic history, not a historical monograph. The images I found limit the scope of the content. I searched private collections and archives for images that best represent all the various communities that occupy space within the term *LGBT* and beyond. In addition, I was limited by page counts. I left out nothing intentionally, and any deficiency within these pages was not deliberate. My hope is that this book will inspire a generation of historians to shed more light and bring more knowledge to the secrets and hidden history of those who identify as LGBT in Utah. LGBT history is a part of Utah history, and we cannot understand where we are as Americans or as Utahns without knowing about our past.

One

A Queer Beginning 1847–1969

The word *queer* has a colorful history and multiple meanings. The past several decades have seen its use increase among the LGBT community as well as by academics. The term is not raced, classed, or gendered and therefore can apply to all sexual minorities. *Queer* has many synonyms—specifically *peculiar, unusual, odd,* or *curious*—and can also be used as a verb.

Salt Lake City is a queer place. Ute, Paiute, Shoshone, and other tribes lived in the area now known as Utah long before the arrival of white colonists. While it would be inappropriate to claim these native peoples as LGBT, their cultures defined family roles, gender roles, and sexualities differently than the European and American colonists who came into their lands.

In 1847, the Brighamite sect of the Church of Jesus Christ of Latter-day Saints imported one of its own queer traditions, the practice of polygamy. Polygamy scandalized many in 19th-century America who found it an affront to morality and decency. But from a global perspective, polygamy is common. Historically, a man having sexual access to many women is not peculiar. What is queer is the way polygamy could give cover to sister wives to form and maintain intimate homoerotic relationships. Women could live in proximity, sharing homes, even beds, and such relationships did not raise the ire of the community. Whether or not these relationships were sexual cannot be known, and it would be irresponsible to claim these women as lesbians. But knowledge of how they lived complicates narratives that insist people of the past could be nothing but heterosexual.

Until 1876, Utah had no law against sodomy. Instead, the law targeted heterosexual fornication while mostly ignoring homosexual activity. Some men were accused of engaging in sodomy; but before passage of a pertinent law, only vigilante justice prevailed. In 1876, the legislature adopted a new penal code that recognized sodomy and included a punishment of five to ten years in the state penitentiary if convicted. The first known sodomy trial occurred in Provo in 1881 but ended with no conviction. The legislature continued to refine state sodomy laws well into the 20th century, eventually including oral sex as an offense. The State Board of Insanity issued a report in 1912 that recommended castration instead of imprisonment for "certain crimes of sexual perversion." In the 1949 case *State v. Cooper*, Justice James Wolfe of the Utah Supreme Court wrote that since homosexuality could be considered a mental illness, the logic of imprisonment "may be seriously questioned." The legislature enacted a psychopathic offender law in 1951 that required mental health screenings for certain criminals, including those charged with sodomy. Under these laws, the men arrested faced time in either a mental institution or prison. In 1969, Utah became the first state to reduce the penalty for consensual sodomy from a felony to a misdemeanor.

Beginning in 1914, Salt Lake City began construction of comfort stations—underground restrooms at busy intersections like State Street and 300 South as well as on Main Street between North Temple and South Temple, and aboveground in Liberty and Pioneer Parks. Comfort stations around the country developed a reputation for immoral and illegal activity because men would often use the locations for sex. Raids by the police into such private/public spaces, including parks and bars where gay and lesbian people met to socialize, escalated in the 1950s and 1960s nationally and in Utah. Despite these threats, gays and lesbians in Utah continued to find one another. As historian Doug Winkler observes, "possible arrest, exposure, and physical violence were persistent fears, but also fostered shared identity and a sense of community in the interest of mutual protection." By 1969, discernable gay and lesbian spaces existed in Salt Lake City, creating the roots for a community to take shape.

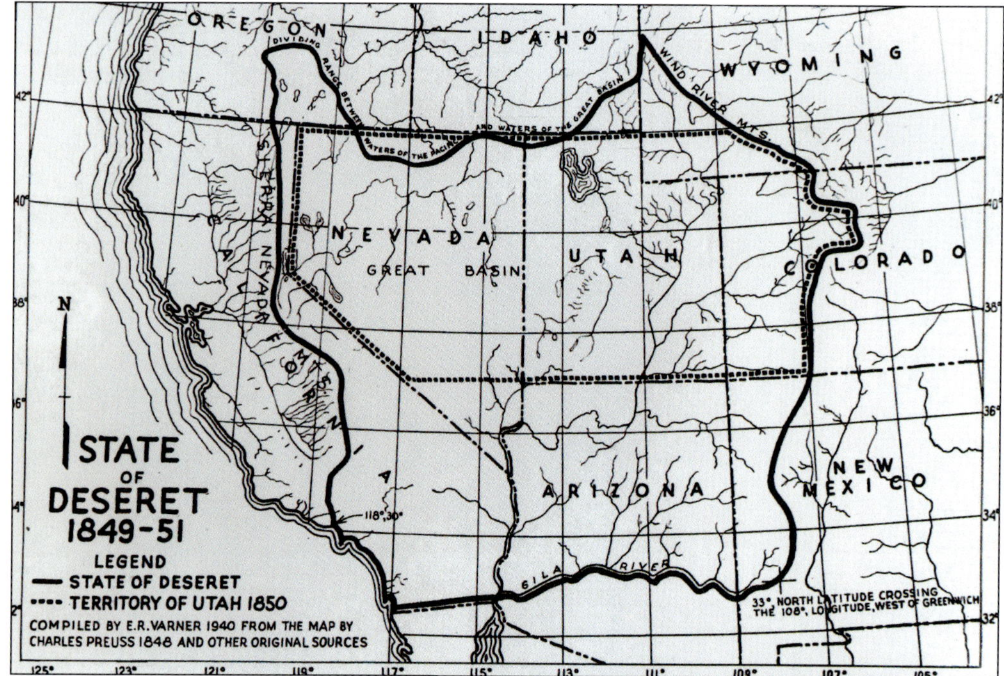

In 1847, Brigham Young led members of the Church of Jesus Christ of Latter-day Saints from Nauvoo, Illinois, across the western border of the United States into what was Mexican territory. A year later, the United States claimed the land at the end of the Mexican-American War. In 1849, Young proposed the creation of the state of Deseret, to be admitted to the Union along with California and New Mexico. Congress never recognized Deseret and instead created the Utah Territory in the Compromise of 1850. Territorial jurisdictions are negotiated and renegotiated over time to create socially constructed boundaries, as evidenced by this 1855 map of western states. The state of Utah took the shape it did as people in positions of power negotiated and renegotiated its boundaries. Lines on maps are socially constructed and reinforced in the same way as sexual and gender identities. Just as lines on maps evolve through a complex process of power struggles, so also do identity categories. (Above, used by permission, Utah State Historical Society; below, courtesy Library of Congress.)

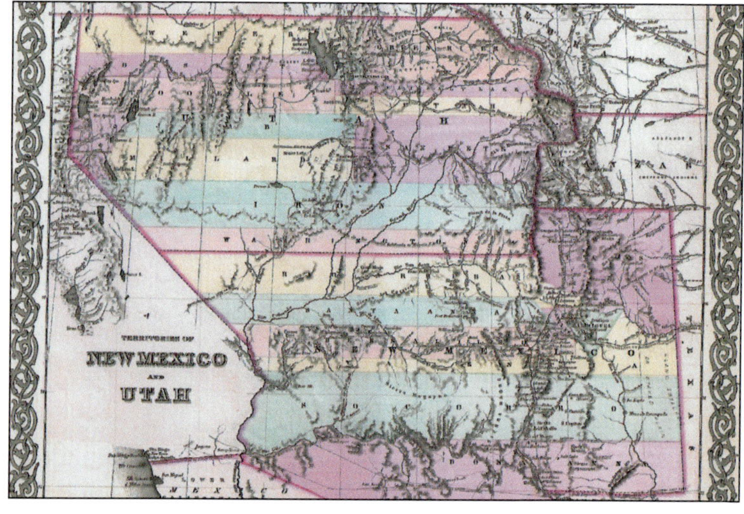

Several Native American tribes lived on the land that became Utah. In Native cultures, traditions surrounding what today might be termed "transgender" were as diverse as Native cultures themselves. When Europeans in the 18th and 19th centuries encountered gender nonconforming Native Americans, they used the term *berdache* to refer to those whose behavior did not fit into European notions of male and female. Since the 1990s, the term *two-spirit* has been widely used. (Used by permission, Utah State Historical Society.)

Brigham Young had 55 wives, which would have been queer by 19th-century American standards since it did not conform to state-sanctioned monogamy. Polygamy is also queer insofar as it could engender intimate same-sex relationships among women that went undetected. (Used by permission, Utah State Historical Society.)

The Utah State Legislature adopted the entire California Penal Code in 1876, which included a statute punishing "the infamous crime against nature." The state revised the law in 1923 to include oral sex. The state sent people convicted of sodomy to the territorial prison (pictured here), which was demolished in the 1950s. Sugarhouse Park is where the prison once stood. (Used by permission, Utah State Historical Society.)

Oscar Wilde, the Sunflower Apostle, embarked on a lecture tour across the United States and Canada in 1882 that took him from New York to California and even Utah, where he met with LDS Church president John Taylor and toured the city. Wilde presented his lecture about the decorative arts in the Salt Lake Theater, located at 100 South State Street. The city did not make a good impression on him; he later remarked the architecture and people were ugly. But Wilde did not make a good impression on the audience, who found him and his public speaking skills lackluster. (Courtesy Library of Congress.)

Sarah Louise "Louie" Felt was the first general president of the children's primary organization for the LDS Church and first wife of Joseph Felt. In 1883, she met May Anderson, who almost became her sister wife. Louie's husband did not marry May, but May moved into their home, where the two women shared a bedroom for 40 years until Louie's death. May never married. It is unknown if their relationship was sexual, but evidence suggests they shared an intense love for one another. (Used by permission, Utah State Historical Society.)

During the 19th century, Regent Street (pictured here), Victoria Alley, and Plumb Alley housed some of the city's brothels, saloons, and parlor houses, where male prostitutes also worked. Madams such as Kate Flint, Helen Blazes, and Lou Wallace were well-known in town. (Used by permission, Utah State Historical Society.)

Brigham Morris Young, son of Brigham Young, performed around the state as Madam Pattirini at the beginning of the 20th century. He was not a drag queen in the modern sense (he was married with children and did not perform as a mode of resistance to a homophobic culture), but he did cross dress and perform around Utah. There is no evidence to suggest he was shamed or shunned for doing so. (Courtesy Church History Library, The Church of Jesus Christ of Latter-day Saints.)

Evan Stephens conducted the Mormon Tabernacle Choir from 1890 to 1916. Stephens never married and spent his life in the company of young men, even naming his friend J. Wallace Packham a principal beneficiary in his will. While it is impossible to know if the relationships were sexual, evidence suggests that Stephens had romantic inclinations towards members of the same sex. (Used by permission, Utah State Historical Society.)

The LDS Church completed the first Deseret Gymnasium in 1910 on the block where the Church Office Building now stands. In the 1950s and 1960s, certain days were sex-segregated and nude swimming was permitted. Though it was not a bathhouse, many gay men reported becoming aware of their same-sex attraction while at the gym. (Used by permission, Utah State Historical Society.)

Auerbach's department store at 300 South State Street reportedly employed the more flamboyant gay men of Salt Lake City in the 1940s and 1950s. The jobs paid little but provided at least a meager living to men who could not or did not want to pass as straight. Men could walk from work a few blocks to bars such as Radio City Lounge, Crystal Lounge, and Tin Angel, public locations where gay men and lesbians met. (Used by permission, Utah State Historical Society.)

By the 1930s, gay men in Salt Lake City knew that Liberty Park was a popular location to clandestinely meet other men. Gay men used certain areas as well as certain restrooms in the evenings for sex. As knowledge of these activities spread outside of gay male circles, law enforcement began to patrol more frequently, often using entrapment to make arrests. (Used by permission, Utah State Historical Society.)

Pres. Heber J. Grant called Joseph F. Smith (pictured here) as patriarch to the LDS Church in 1942. When evidence came before the First Presidency about Smith's homosexual relationship with a young man, he was released in 1946. Smith moved to Hawaii, where he was not permitted to speak in church or have church callings. In 1957, Pres. David O. McKay allowed him to return to church activity. (Used by permission, Utah State Historical Society.)

The Missouri Café operated next to the Western Furniture store (right) at 147 South State Street, but a few months after this image was taken in 1947, the Radio City Lounge replaced the café. Opening in 1948, Radio City Lounge became known as a downtown bar where gays and lesbians could meet. Police chief W. Cleon Skousen often raided the bar as its reputation as a location for gays and lesbians became better known. (Used by permission, Utah State Historical Society.)

Slightly obscured by the wreath, the sign for the Crystal Lounge is visible. By the early 1950s, the bar at 174 South State Street had become another location for gay men and lesbians to meet. In 1957, a publicized arrest of a man from Idaho on "morals charges" exposed the existence of locations where gays and lesbians assembled. Fearing exposure and being shut down, the owners withdrew their welcome of gay and lesbian customers. (Used by permission, Utah State Historical Society.)

W. Cleon Skousen (left), a prominent conservative writer and political theorist, was a staunch anticommunist and supporter of the John Birch Society. He left the FBI in 1951 and began working at BYU as director of public services and assistant professor of speech. Adiel F. Stewart, who served as mayor of Salt Lake City from 1956 to 1960, appointed Skousen as chief of police in 1956. As chief of police, Skousen launched a crusade against "moral perverts" by raiding bars, suspending liquor licenses, and strictly enforcing sex crime laws. He used polygraph tests when hiring policemen that asked invasive questions to weed out applicants "involved in promiscuous immorality or homosexuality." In one of Utah's more intriguing political confrontations, Salt Lake City mayor J. Bracken Lee removed Skousen as chief of police in 1960, saying that Skousen used the police force for "scaring his enemies and protecting his friends." Here, Channel 2 newsman Doug Mitchell (right) listens as Skousen speaks about law enforcement in the city and his thoughts on being fired. (Used by permission, Utah State Historical Society.)

By the mid-20th century, local law enforcement made a concerted effort to rid the city of "sex deviates." Legislatures passed laws known as "sexual psychopath laws" in 26 states by 1967 to protect the public from a rising wave of alleged sex crimes. These laws more often than not targeted gay men. Men arrested in known cruising areas such as bus or train stations faced time in either the new prison built in Draper in 1951 (pictured here) or the state mental institution (pictured below). (Used by permission, Utah State Historical Society.)

Definitions of sexual psychopath laws varied but often included a premise that some types of sexual offenses, including homosexuality, were rooted in mental illness. Statutes stipulated that sex offenders be treated by a psychiatrist who could certify if the man arrested was mentally ill. Based on the evaluation, judges would send some men to the state mental hospital in Provo for an indefinite period of time for treatment. (Used by permission, Utah State Historical Society.)

Mildred J. Berryman was born in Salt Lake City in 1901. She worked as a researcher, writer, photographer, and stenographer. She identified as a lesbian and during the 1930s wrote a thesis for Temple Bar College in Seattle titled "The Psychological Phenomena of the Homosexual." She gathered data on 23 lesbians (including herself) and nine gay men whom she met through the Bohemian Club in Salt Lake City. She stopped working on the thesis in 1939 and never completed it. She died in 1972. (Courtesy *Mineralogist*.)

Mormon pioneers constructed an adobe building over the hot springs at 840 North 300 West in 1850. The city acquired the location in 1921, built a Mission Revival structure over the pools, and called it the Warm Springs Municipal Bath. The name was changed to Warm Springs Plunge in 1932. A 1937 thesis titled "The Invert Personality" notes how inverts (homosexuals) used the space to meet for sex. (Used by permission, Utah State Historical Society.)

In 1949, Gov. J. Bracken Lee organized the Utah Committee on the Sex Offender and the Community to address concerns over perceived increases in sex offenses. Lee appointed Arthur Beeley, a criminologist and dean of the University of Utah School of Social Work, to chair the committee. Beeley recommended that new laws against sex offenders were unnecessary and instead emphasized treatment as opposed to incarceration for "sexual deviants." In 1960, Lee became mayor of Salt Lake City. (Used by permission, Utah State Historical Society.)

The tension between Mormonism and homosexuality was apparent as early as the 1950s. Allen Drury published his political thriller *Advise and Consent* in 1959. The novel includes a prominent Mormon character, US senator Brigham Anderson from Idaho, who is revealed to be gay. Knowing his career is ruined and that voters would never forgive him, he commits suicide. The novel plays on prominent Cold War themes linking homosexuality and communism. (Courtesy Penguin Random House.)

Inspired by Finocchio's Club in San Francisco, the Tin Angel opened at 340 South State Street in 1966. The Tin Angel used female impersonation as a novelty for the mostly straight audience and billed the Missfits as "Salt Lake City's most unusual show." This is an early example of how business owners used homosexuality as entertainment for heterosexual audiences. (Both, courtesy Doug Winkler.)

Two

Gay Liberation in Utah 1969–1983

Riots on June 28 and 29, 1969, at a Greenwich Village bar, the Stonewall Inn, sent shock waves through cities with large gay populations. The idea that gender and sexual minorities could physically fight back against the police and also fight more broadly against a homophobic culture seemed revolutionary. Although the relevance of Stonewall was not immediately apparent, it has in the decades following taken on historic significance as a call to arms for gender and sexual minorities to fight oppression as well as a historical moment that signaled a change in consciousness about sexual minorities' status as citizens. Post-Stonewall Gay Liberation groups envisioned a national discourse that affirmed their worth and dignity rather than one that demoralized, shamed, jailed, beat, and humiliated them. These ideas and eventually the organizations that promoted them appeared in Salt Lake City in subtle but significant ways in the 1970s.

The gay and lesbian community in Salt Lake City came out in the 1970s. Perky's, a lesbian bar, opened in 1970. A congregation of the Metropolitan Community Church began in 1972 and began publishing the *Cricket*, the first gay-affirming newsletter in Utah. The following year, Joe Redburn opened the state's first official gay bar, the Sun Tavern, on South Temple and 400 West. It became the preeminent location for gay and lesbian people in the city to take refuge, meet one another, dance, and publicize information about current events, news, and social groups. Nikki Boyer opened Sisters just south of the Sun Tavern in 1975. On June 28, 1975, the Gay Community Service Center, the first of its kind in Utah, published the *Gayzette*, a newsletter written by and for the gay community. That same month, the center sponsored Gay Freedom Day in City Creek Canyon. Jeff's Gym, at 727 West 1700 South, one of several bathhouses in the city, opened in 1976. The Imperial Court of Utah (later renamed the Royal Court of the Golden Spike Empire), the oldest nonprofit serving the gay community in the state, crowned its first emperor and empress in 1976. In 1977, Babs DeLay published the *Rocky Mountain Woman*. That same year, Matthew Price helped organize a group for gay and lesbian Mormons called Affirmation: Gay Mormons United and the Gay Student Union filed formal paperwork to become an official club at the University of Utah. A lesbian collective, Women Aware, formed in 1979 and established a food co-op and bookstore called 20 Rue Jacob.

The increased visibility of gays and lesbians in the city led to increased condemnations, specifically from LDS Church leaders. During this decade, antigay rhetoric used by church leaders intensified and became more explicit. However, as Cloy Jenkins writes in *Prologue: An Examination of Mormon Attitudes Towards Homosexuality* in 1978, "the days of passive acceptance of humiliation and discrimination are over." The gay and lesbian community in Salt Lake City would never again be silent.

The
CRICKET
Metropolitan Community Church, Salt Lake City, Utah

P. O. Box 11607
VOLUME I
NUMBER 16
NOVEMBER 26, 1972

740 South 7th East
Phone: 328-1517

CRICKET TRACKS
As editor of the SLC newsletter vehicle, may I urge you to help stuff the Cricket Cage with original articles. I hope to see the Cricket a newsy, NOW info paper. You will note as of this issue and in the future, staff editors being added, ie: food editor, medical editor, foot note editor, book nook editor, etc., ALL depending upon YOUR response. I shall try to stay within the universal concepts of an editor, that of: being uniformative, biased, quick to censor and controversial. Remember, a Cricket's bite can be worse than a seagull's beak.

THANK YOU, SEATTLE, MCC
SLC-MCC has always been fortunate in receiving the blessings and well wishes of the great men of our Fellowship. Two weeks ago Sunday, we were greatful for the visit of Rev. Robert Sirico (MCC, Seattle). His very form & graciousness restored the faith in ourselves that so often gets buried as we are tried from day to day. We are extremely fond of Pastor Sirico. He will always occupy a special place in our hearts as one of the great men in Christ and a true SHAKER of the foundations. A lovely reception was held for him in the home of Dick & Algin. The entire congregation responded enthusiastically to his pastoral warmth as well as his very human grace. God be with Pastor Sirico.

— Delores L.

SHERE: HELP! WHAT?
For the home body type, your Watkins Products Represanative, Cecil M. Cooper. 359-4871

How about some transportation? 1964 4-door Mercury, Gd. condition. $395.00. Bob Macier 328-2700

For those who like fine or different clothes. Your local tailor and designer. Cecil M. Cooper 359-4871

Tax Service - Cecil M. Cooper 359-4871

The Metropolitan Community Church (MCC), founded in California by Rev. Troy Perry in 1968, established a congregation in Utah in 1972. Led by Pastor Richard Groh and later Pastor Alice Jones, the MCC published the *Cricket*, the first gay-affirming newsletter in the state. (Courtesy Utah Stonewall Historical Society.)

Steve Jones reopened the Cosmic Aeroplane Bookstore on the corner of South Temple and 400 West. He is shown here standing next to his business in 1972. Several gay and lesbian bars opened on this corner in the mid-1970s. In addition to the Sun Tavern, Nikki Boyer opened Sisters and later Uptown Place. The Rail opened on the same block. (Courtesy Steve Jones.)

In 1973, Joe Redburn (standing) opened the Sun Tavern, the first gay bar in the state with a sign. Perky's had opened in 1970 on North Temple as a bar for women but was more discreet. Bars in the gay and lesbian movement have done more than just provide a place to drink; they have also functioned as miniature community centers. Gay bars in Salt Lake City were no different. Throughout the 1970s, the Sun Tavern became the foremost social gathering location for the community. The Sun Tavern moved to 200 South and 600 West after the city bought the original location and demolished it to build the Delta Center in 1990. A tornado destroyed the second location in 1999. (Courtesy Utah Stonewall Historical Society.)

Rebecca Terry Heal, Kristen Merrill, and Michelle Nunley sang as backup singers to local musicians in the 1970s. In 1981, they became known as the Saliva Sisters after they performed in garbage bags singing songs about bras, bidets, and fiber. They are longtime allies to the gay and lesbian community and are seen here performing at the Sun Tavern in 1983. (Courtesy Scott Stites.)

Nikki Boyer had been involved in the lesbian and gay community before moving to Utah in the late 1960s. In Salt Lake City, she worked as a bartender in several gay bars in town, including the Sun Tavern, helped organized the first gay and lesbian beer kegger in 1975, and opened several bars. She has been a longtime activist in Utah, including serving on the Utah Pride Center Board of Directors. (Courtesy David Daniels.)

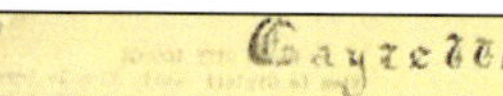

GAY COMMUNITY SERVICE CENTER, SALT LAKE CITY, UTAH NO. 0 JUNE 28, 1975

EVENTS...

- SUNSTONES Picnic...July 29 outing at B.A.B. $3.00 donation includes food and beer. The Sunstones are a soft-ball team composed of gay women who play in two leagues. Donations will raise funds for jackets and out-of-state tournaments.
- G.C.S.C. General meeting every Monday evening at 7:30 or as posted at the Center.
- Volunteer In-Service-Training for crisis intervention : Wednesday at 7:30, July 2. Anyone interested please come.
- G.C.S.C. (Gay Community Services Center) outing is scheduled for July 24. This one will be even better than the last with more entertainment, sales of art, photography, crafts; more contests ; more "happenings." Make it happen July 24. Get details at the Center, bars and churches.

announcements...

- Donations to the Center may be made to Billee. Checks may be made payable to "G.C.S.C."
- Donations of office furnishings are still needed by the Center. Thanks to everyone who has donated items and time to making the Center so comfortable and attractive.
- Submission of articles and opinions (pseudonyms and initials will be used unless your name is requested) are invited by the Gayzette. Submit them by the third Saturday each month (July 19 this month.) Drop them in the door slot at the Center after office hours.
- The Gayzette is soliciting ads.

CONTEST WINNERS...

- Newspaper name: GAYZETTE
  Winner: Steve J.
- Logo: (to right)
  Winner: Will E.

- Motto: "Probitas Amare" (The Right to Love)
  Winner: James H.

THE CENTER IS IN ACTION !!

Jason S. was a drop-in at the Center on the verge of attempting suicide after a previous try several years ago. He is in his 20's, has been in the Salt Lake area for 6 months. In that period of time he has found no companionship or acknowledgment. He is an attractive guy who had been active in theatre in New York. Here he is employed at a prison where he has daily approaches but cannot ethically respond to prisoners advances. The combined effect of these frustrations plus a broken relationship not quite left behind in New York brought Jason to the crisis point.
At the Center he was able to rap and to learn of the alternatives available within our Community. He has made acquaintances on a non - sexual basis, appeared on a local radio talk show to tell how the Center had helped him, and as a degree holder in psychology is preparing to help others through the Center.

Billee and Dorothy appeared on Joe Redburn's KUER-FM radio last-of-a-series talk-show on June 21. They did a fine job of presenting the Center's Services to their listeners and answering the questions of callers.

CANYON PARTY IN JUNE A GREAT SUCCESS

The Canyon Party sponsored by GCSC was an overwhelming success. Many people have said they were not aware of it and missed it. Yet, there were better than 400 people in attendance. The most overwhelming factor, however, was the humanity which everyone expressed toward one another, especially toward those with whom they felt estranged.

The Center wants to thank everyone for his or her donation and to all those people who helped to make the event such a great success. Special thanks go to Larry S. who is missed by all of us who saw him work so hard. Also to be thanked are those who cooked, cleaned the areas, drove the taxies, parked, played, donated time,money and talent, and to everyone who cared enough to be there to join brothers and sisters in joyful festivities.

D.S.

The printing was donated and done by: The Feminist Women's Health Center, 328-3032, a woman-controlled health center dedicated to reclaiming our bodies from the medical profession. Call for information.

The Gay Community Service Center published the first gay community newsletter in June 1975. Originally titled *Gayzette*, the publication promoted the efforts of the center to build and unify the gay and lesbian community through picnics, meetings, and social functions. The publication proved to be a vital tool, but the center only published a few issues. (Courtesy University of Utah.)

The Gay Community Service Center continued to publish a newsletter under the name the *Salt Lick* after the *Gayzette* stopped printing. Unlike similar underground newsletters published in other cities during these years, some issues were courageously signed by editor Babs DeLay. (Courtesy Utah Stonewall Historical Society.)

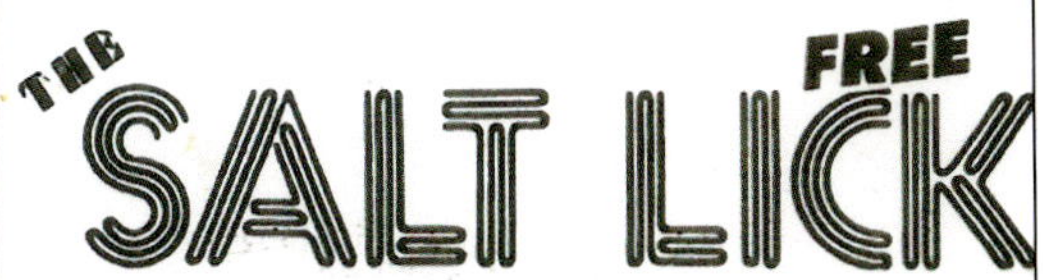

THE SALT LICK FREE

The Voice of the Gay Community Vol.2 No.2 May 1976
Salt Lake City, Utah

Center is still alive and kicking

As many of you may already know, the Gay [...]unity Service Center is no longer at 11 South 4th West. Due to financial difficulties, [...] lack of support from the Gay Community in [...]ral, the Center has had to reduce expenses [...] minimum. "Call-forwarding" has replaced [...] answering service for the 24 hour crisis-[...]. However, all calls are still taken by [...]one at all hours of the day or night, to help [a]ssist the caller.

The heat, power and light bills have been [r]eplaced with the cost of a postoffice box [...]er.

Meetings will continue, and will be pub-[...]zed in advance and held at various institu-[...]s, as well as out of doors, weather permit-[...]. Long-range goals presently are to open a Center, at a location away from all bars, in [di]gnified location with facilities which will [hope]fully encourage and attract active partici-[pati]on in the Center. All of this takes time, [ene]rgy and devotion to our cause. We will [over]come.

Present plans for the immediate future are [m]ost canyon parties, weather cooperating [...]r in the season, and study is being given to [work]shops for the gay and straight communities, hopefully better understand the problems each [...] in a mutual cooperation to learn to live in [harm]ony together.

The Center has need of individuals who put [the] good and well-being of the Gay Community above [thei]r own personal interests. We have quite [enou]gh of the ego-trip individuals, who cannot [or w]ill not work with others, who throw their [...]s to the wind as soon as diversity rises.. [We n]eed sincere and dedicated people, those who [...] their heads on their shoulders and a solid [...]ing and firm foundation. We need and demand people who are gay and are proud of it, prou[d of] their own minds, but not necessarily to the point of flaunting it openly. We encourage dignity and pride.

VD Outbreak Threatens

Painful though it may be, one of the [...] truths of the gay life is that with it come[s] risk of venereal disease. With promiscuity comes increased danger of disease, and unte[...] VD can be deadly, no pun intended.

Recently, the Gay Community Board of Directors was asked to meet with Tom Nelder[man] from the Utah Health Department. It was stated that an outbreak of syphilis is bein[g] noted, and an alarming rate is being found [in] the gay population. This outbreak could soo[n] reach epidemic proportions.

VD clinics are available, free of charg[e] as well as through your own personal doctor. The main thing is to get a blood test to mak[e] sure, positive or negative. Mr. Niederman asked that anyone suspect of VD offer themse[lves] for 'screening', which makes the testing geared to syphilis. A follow-up and another blood-test is needed, 30 days after the firs[t] test. Two negative tests and steady breathi[ng] may resume.

Plans are to set up clinics at some of [the] bars, and also at some of the churches, coop[era]tion forthcoming. Word of these clinics wil[l] be advertised, and all opportunity will be [...] to curb this disease before it becomes rampa[nt]. Meanwhile, if anyone suspects VD, remember y[our] own future is at stake. Warning has been posted. Take it from here.

THE OPEN DOO[R]

[...]r 1976. Address: PO Box 6077, SLC 84106 --The voice of the SLC Gay Commun[ity]

EDITORIAL COMMENT

[Af]ter some months of obvious silence, the [co]mmunity of Salt Lake City has become [...]e again.

[We] are now known as the GAY SERVICE [COALIT]ION, incorporated by the State of Utah, [a]nd respectable in the eyes of some [a]t least, and ready to go forward.

[We] are an outgrowth of the group of gay-[...]ed persons who meet at the Monday [...]gs (more information call 533-0927).

[We] are aligned with no business firm, [...] no preference to any special-interest but we are interested in the gay [...] first, last and always.

[Th]is paper, hopefully, will be published [mo]re or less regular basis, and present [...]s written and submitted by the gay [commun]ity. We will carry advertising, and [...] permitting, find a professional [...]r for pictures and paste-ups for ads.

[Th]e Coalition needs support, moral and [financ]ial types. The telephone line will [ope]rative 24 hours a day if volunteers are [suffic]ient in numbers to man the line. This [...]ine has proven its' value in the past, [...] hope to continue it in the future. [Com]ments and opinions during these [convers]ations are supremely confidential and [tr]ained and proven reliable individuals [...] answering the phone. The phone [m]oney, we have no steady income, so [...] we solicit whatever financial support [...] give us.

[Soc]ial events will be planned for get-[togeth]ers and fun. These events will be [announ]ced in the OPEN DOOR, as they emerge.

[Th]e COALITION asks your participation [...] survey in this issue, to better [...]e ourselves, and our progress. We [...]r cooperation, and welcome suggestions. [...] new and fresh ideas, articles for [...]er, written in good taste with [...]ty if desired. Our primary goal is [...]eve public recognition that the gay [commun]ity is upstanding and respectable and [not] a second-rate citizen. With a lot of [...]d dedication, this can become an [estab]lished fact.

GAY RIGHTS AND POLITICAL HONESTY
--By Steve Trotter

"But how do we know you truly [...] in gay rights if you're not gay yourse[lf?]"

That is a question (and a leg[...] one) which I have been asked on severa[l] occasions while campaigning for the US [...]

First, let's take a look at t[he] other two parties.

The Platform of the Democrats [...] even mention the rights of gay people, [let] alone defend those rights. As I write[...] the Republicans have not yet drafted t[heir] Platform, but we all know they won't h[ave] anything worthwhile to offer.

Now let's take a look at our [...]

The Libertarian Party is the [...] significant party with a platform plan[k] defending gay rights.

In the Preamble to our platfo[rm we] say: "We hold that all individuals ha[ve the] right to live in whatever manner they [...] so long as they do not forcibly interf[ere] with the equal right of others to live [in] whatever manner they choose."

Not specific enough? From th[e] body of the Platform: "In particular, [we] advocate...The repeal of all laws rega[rding] consensual sexual relations, including prostitution and solicitation, and the cessation of state oppression and harr[assment] of homosexual men and women, that they be accorded their full rights as indiv[iduals]." (Page 1, plank 2)

More? Okay: 'We call for th[e end of] the Defense Department practice of dis[...] armed forces personnel for homosexual [...] We further call for retraction of all [...] honorable discharges for such reasons [...] deletion of such information from mili[tary] files." (Page 4, plank 12.)

Still more? "No individual r[ights] should be denied or abridged by the la[ws of] the United States or any state or loca[lity on] account of sex, race, color, creed, ag[e], national origin, or sexual preference. [We] condemn bigotry as irrational and repu[gnant]." (Page 5, plank 15)

(Cont'd, next page)

Bob Waldrop became the pastor of the MCC in 1977. In 1979, he purchased the *Open Door*, which had been publishing issues since 1976. The title of the paper referenced the opening of the closet door and encouraged gays and lesbians to come out. The paper covered local and national news, politics, and commentary on the treatment of gays and lesbians in Utah. Waldrop received numerous death threats and hate mail for publishing the paper, which ceased publication in 1981. (Courtesy University of Utah.)

After Lt. Gov. David Monson rescinded permission for the MCC to hold a dance at the state capitol in April 1977, Pastor Bob Waldrop (pictured) sued, alleging religious discrimination. In *Metropolitan Community Church v. Monson*, the Third District Court ruled in favor of the MCC. In addition to his duties as pastor, Waldrop dealt with growing violence towards gay and lesbian people, including the murder of gay activist Tony Adams and break-ins at the MCC office. He helped organize the demonstration against Anita Bryant, organized vigils, spoke to the media about challenges facing the gay and lesbian community, and published the *Open Door.* (Courtesy University of Utah.)

Robert I. McQueen was a prominent gay Mormon, activist, and writer. He graduated from the University of Utah with a degree in journalism and moved to San Francisco in the early 1970s. McQueen worked as a writer for the *Advocate*, the largest national gay and lesbian newspaper at the time. He wrote several stories about religion and homosexuality, specifically gay Mormons, and served as the editor of the *Advocate* from 1975 to 1985. McQueen passed away in 1989 from AIDS-related complications. (Courtesy B. Jane Hudson.)

Stephan Zacharias (going by the name Matthew Price), along with several Mormon and ex-Mormon gays and lesbians, founded Affirmation: Gay Mormons United in 1977 in Salt Lake City. Paul Mortensen formed the Los Angeles chapter in 1978. Here, Rev. Troy Perry, founder of the Metropolitan Community Church, stands next to Mortensen at the 1979 Los Angeles Pride Parade. In 1980, the organization changed names to Affirmation: Gay and Lesbian Mormons. (Courtesy Affirmation.)

Members of Affirmation: Gay Mormons United attended the first March on Washington for Lesbian and Gay Rights on October 14, 1979. This first march drew an estimated crowd of between 75,000 and 125,000 people and helped create the sense of a national gay rights movement. Gay rights activists such as writer Audre Lorde, Leonard Matlovich, Rev. Troy Perry, and Rep. Ted Weiss (D-New York) spoke at the march. (Courtesy Affirmation.)

Anita Bryant made headlines in 1977 with her Save Our Children campaign. She portrayed herself as one of the "silent majority" who feared adverse effects on children from Gay Liberation. When she performed at the Utah State Fairpark in 1977, the Salt Lake Coalition for Human Rights, led by Pastor Bob Waldrop, protested the event. This protest marked the first time members of the gay community demonstrated publicly for their rights as citizens. (Courtesy *Salt Lake Tribune*.)

After the protest against Anita Bryant, Pastor Bob Waldrop led a vigil for 200 people in Memory Grove. Bob Evans (left) and Greg Garcia attended. The vigil commemorated the murders of three gay men in Utah the previous June and included speeches by Waldrop; Bob Kunst, a gay rights activist from Miami; Shirley Pedler from the ACLU of Utah; and Rep. Jeff Fox. A canister of tear gas dispersed the crowd as the vigil ended. (Courtesy *Salt Lake Tribune*.)

Reed Payne, a Brigham Young University psychology professor, gave an antigay lecture at BYU in 1977. A gay student at BYU, Cloy Jenkins, with the help of a few others, wrote a 52-page response to the lecture that called for a "well reasoned dialogue" on the topic of Mormonism and homosexuality. The *Open Door* published the essay over three issues. Jenkins published his rebuttal anonymously under the title *Prologue* in 1978. (Courtesy L. Young.)

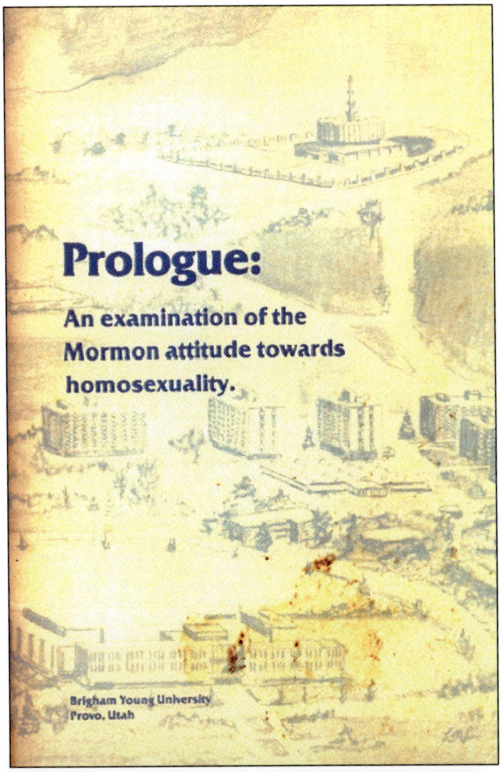

Prologue:

An examination of the Mormon attitude towards homosexuality.

Brigham Young University
Provo, Utah

The Imperial Court of Utah formed as a social group for the gay community and today is the oldest gay-rights group in the state. It crowned its first emperor, Pepper Prespentt (left), and first empress, Deanna, at the Rusty Bell in 1976. Pepper was the first lesbian emperor and continues to be involved in the organization, which changed names to the Royal Court of the Golden Spike Empire in 1981. (Courtesy Scott Stites.)

Steve Jones and Sherm Clow opened the Cosmic Aeroplane in 1967 at 871 East 900 South. It moved to various locations over the years, including this one at 366 South West Temple. It defined itself as an alternative bookstore that sold underground newspapers, beads, records, jewelry, and paraphernalia. In addition to mainstream books, it sold gay-themed books and magazines, advertised in the *Salt Lick* and the *Open Door*, and attracted a clientele of poets, musicians, artists, antiwar protestors, gay rights activists, and feminists. (Courtesy Steve Jones.)

LESBIAN & GAY STUDENT UNION'S (LGSU!)

COFFEE HOUSE

UNION BUILDING
FACULTY LOUNGE
'U OF U'

(friday) november 9, 1979:
7:00-11:00 pm.

Refreshments - Entertainment

The L.G.S.U. will be presenting its second Coffee House. This will be held the second Friday of each month to provide an informal atmosphere for socialising and entertainment; primarily musical this month!

For more information: 322-5010 or 364-5886

The Gay Student Union formed at the University of Utah in 1977, although it had existed informally before then. By 1979, members changed the name to the Lesbian and Gay Student Union (LGSU). This group sponsored educational activities for gay and nongay students, held weekly meetings, wrote a newsletter, and sought to create an atmosphere of acceptance for lesbian and gay students on campus. Monthly "coffee house" meetings allowed students to meet and socialize. (Courtesy University of Utah.)

Members of Affirmation, led by Randy Smith, demonstrate in front of Temple Square during the General Conference of the LDS Church in October 1981. "We are human beings like everyone else," Smith told the press. According to news reports, this was the first time the Salt Lake City Council granted a permit to a gay rights group to demonstrate on public property. Men carried signs that read, "We are Your Children" and chanted, "Two, four, six eight, gay is just as good as straight!" About 30 people participated. (Courtesy Garry Bryant.)

After police discovered what gay men in town referred to as "Bare Ass Beach" or "Bare Bum Beach" in 1982, they began issuing citations and making arrests. Men used the secluded white-sand beach, located northeast of where the old Saltair Pavilion (pictured here in 1900) once stood, to sunbathe nude and cruise for sex. Deputy David Bishop told the press that "prominent businessmen" as well as men with wives and children had been ticketed at the beach. (Courtesy Library of Congress.)

In 1983, the MCC branch renamed itself the Resurrection Metropolitan Community Church. It met in this building at 823 South 600 East with Bruce Barton as pastor. The building is still used as a place of worship by the Sacred Light of Christ Church, an LGBT-affirming congregation. (Author's collection.)

Trevor Southey was born in Zimbabwe. He studied art in Sussex, England, and Durban, South Africa. After converting to the LDS Church, he moved to Provo, where he earned two degrees from Brigham Young University and eventually taught there. He was a prominent artist when he came out as gay in 1984, leading to his divorce and excommunication. His honesty and art inspired a generation of students, artists, and gay Mormons. Southey passed away in 2015. (Courtesy Elaine Walton.)

Three

Activism in the Time of AIDS 1983–1992

Although it is impossible to know with certainty when HIV arrived in the state, the Utah Department of Health confirmed the first cases of AIDS in 1983 and began compiling statistics that year. Byron Haslam of the state's Bureau of Communicable Disease made the first public acknowledgement of AIDS in Utah on July 21, 1983. The state allocated no money to the epidemic but did receive a grant from the Centers for Disease Control in May 1986—$117,286 to create programs aimed at controlling and preventing the spread of HIV/AIDS. However, state epidemiologist Craig Nichols refused to use any of the money to distribute information on safe sex, including condom use. He told the press in 1986, "We'll do the things we know we can do and are acceptable. And other groups will have to fill in where they think there's a deficit." By March 1987, the Utah Department of Health recorded 60 AIDS cases, of which 43 people had died.

During the early years of the epidemic, Dr. Kristen Ries, an infections disease specialist, treated the majority of Utahns with HIV/AIDS. In 1981, Dr. Ries came to Utah, where she became a local expert on the perplexing new disease. By 1985, she was treating 50 people who were living with HIV/AIDS in her private practice. Dr. Ries had admitting privileges to Holy Cross Hospital, where she met RN Maggie Snyder, who by 1987 primarily treated people with HIV/AIDS. (Snyder began course work to become a physician assistant in 1988 specifically to help Dr. Ries with the growing number of people under her medical care.) In 1987, RN Grace Blodgett spearheaded the creation of Med III, the state's first 10-bed inpatient unit for people with AIDS, managed by RN Pam Bruce at Holy Cross Hospital. That same year, Sister Linda Bellemore, also a registered nurse, provided care to people with AIDS under the Continuity of Care program. By July 1986, Dr. Ries saw the disease spreading in Utah and told members of the Salt Lake Rotary Club in a speech that over 400 Utahns tested positive for HIV, the virus that leads to AIDS, making the disease a major epidemic in the state.

Grassroots efforts to assist people with AIDS were under way by 1985. Dr. Patty Reagan founded the Salt Lake AIDS Foundation; Duane Dawson, a nurse, formed AIDS Project Utah; David Sharpton founded the People With AIDS Coalition of Utah; Father Don Bramble started a support group for people with AIDS; and Dick Dotson founded Horizon House. The Royal Court of the Golden Spike Empire, a nonprofit pageant system established in 1976 to serve the needs of Utah's gay and lesbian community, began fundraising for people with AIDS in 1986. Under Emperor Scott Stites, the Royal Court raised over $10,000 from various gay community groups in Salt Lake City. Stites also created the first AIDS Awareness Week in Utah, a tradition observed to this day.

In the midst of the fear about AIDS, members of the gay and lesbian community continued to organize and live their lives openly. Gay Pride Day continued throughout the 1980s, and in 1986, the Gay and Lesbian Community Council formed; it met monthly to discuss activities and concerns facing the community. By 1991, a chapter of Queer Nation formed in Utah with the stated purpose of promoting queer visibility and fighting homophobia that had increased due to the stigma attached to HIV/AIDS.

When Ogden resident Clair Harward confessed to his bishop in 1985 that he was gay and dying from AIDS, the bishop excommunicated him and told him not to return to church for fear he would spread AIDS in the congregation. This photograph of Harward showing his body covered in Kaposi's sarcoma is the first photograph published in the *Salt Lake Tribune* of someone with AIDS. Harward passed away in March 1986 at the age of 26. (Courtesy *Salt Lake Tribune*.)

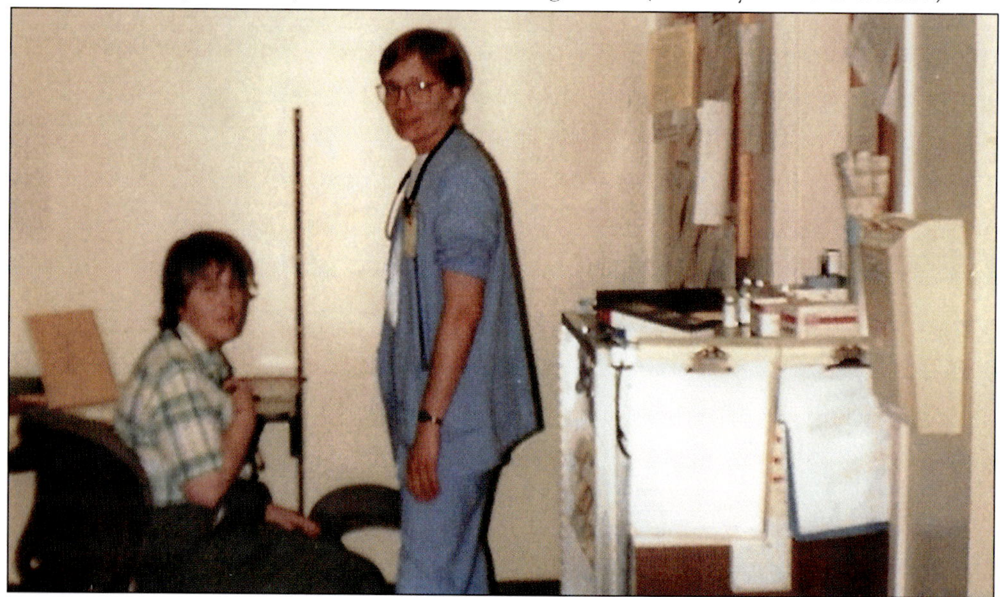

At a time when other doctors turned people with AIDS away, Dr. Kristen Ries (left) and RN Maggie Snyder were among the few health-care providers to treat people with HIV/AIDS in Utah in the 1980s. Known for the compassionate care they gave their patients, they accepted drop-ins at their clinic, made house calls, and accepted clients who did not have insurance. Their efforts ensured that many people died with dignity and as comfortably as possible. (Courtesy Maggie Snyder.)

Maggie Snyder grew up in Houston, Texas, but in the early 1980s moved to Salt Lake City, where she began working as a nurse at Holy Cross Hospital, the first hospital to admit and treat people with AIDS. In 1988, Dr. Kristen Ries asked if she would consider becoming a physician assistant and then coming to work with her, which Snyder did. In 1994, the women moved their practice and 500 patients with HIV to the University of Utah Clinic 1A. (Courtesy Maggie Snyder.)

Pictured here as the grand marshal of the Pride Parade in 1995, Dr. Kristen Ries grew up in Pennsylvania, where she graduated cum laude from Women's Medical College of Pennsylvania. She arrived in Utah in 1981 as an infectious disease specialist. For nearly a decade, she worked long hours as one of the only doctors in the state to treat people with HIV/AIDS. Organizers of the Utah Pride Festival have awarded a deserving person from the community with the Dr. Kristen Ries Award since 1987, with Dr. Ries as the first recipient. (Courtesy Maggie Snyder.)

Grace Blodgett, an RN at Holy Cross Hospital, helped create the first 10-bed inpatient unit for people with HIV/AIDS, known as Med III, in 1987. Nuns working at the hospital included Sister Linda Bellemore, Sister Olivia Marie Hutcheson, and Sister Joan Marie Steadman. The nuns and the nurses (pictured here) all served people with AIDS through direct care or support services. In a speech in 1990, Dr. Patty Reagan recalled that "the nuns who worked there were great. They were generous, loving, kind. Sister Linda was a major, major supporter of the community. (Courtesy Maggie Snyder.)

This 1986 issue of *Triangle* shows some of the people responsible for creating organizations to address the growing AIDS epidemic in Utah. Dr. Patty Reagan started the Salt Lake AIDS Foundation (later called the Utah AIDS Foundation), Fr. Don Bramble started a support group for people with AIDS, and nurse Duane Dawson cofounded AIDS Project Utah. (Courtesy University of Utah.)

David Sharpton and Tom Lindsey cofounded the People with AIDS Coalition of Utah in the mid-1980s. Early organizers of the movement in San Francisco used the name "People with AIDS" to reject the label of "AIDS victim" or "AIDS patient" as the media often reported. Organizers focused on spreading a message of empowerment to people with AIDS and offering support, as expressed on this flier. The coalition still operates in Utah. (Courtesy University of Utah.)

Doctors diagnosed David Sharpton with AIDS in 1985. Under his leadership, the People with AIDS Coalition of Utah began a high-profile public information campaign to raise awareness of the disease in Utah. In 1988, Sharpton addressed the 7,000-member US Conference of Mayors on behalf of the National Association of People with AIDS. He was also the subject of a PBS documentary titled *Remembering David*. He passed away from complications related to AIDS in 1992. (Courtesy University of Utah.)

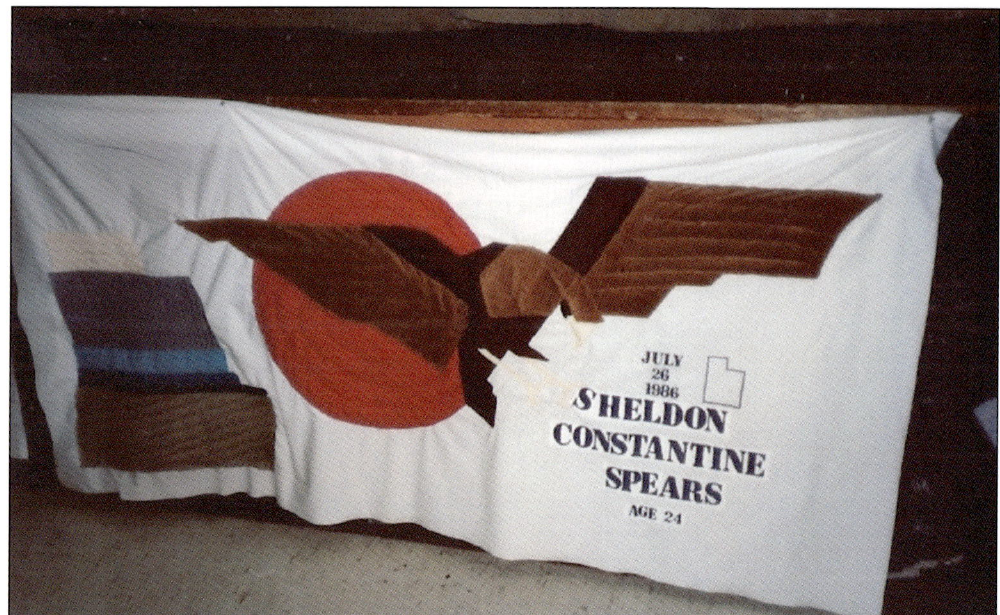

Doctors diagnosed Sheldon Spears with AIDS in 1985. He became one of Utah's first outspoken AIDS activists and campaigned for an AIDS outreach program and funding for education and support for people with AIDS. He passed away from complications related to AIDS in 1986 and was remembered in this AIDS Memorial Quilt panel. (Courtesy Maggie Snyder.)

On May 25, 1986, the Royal Court of the Golden Spike Empire held its annual coronation at the Salt Palace, where it crowned a new emperor and empress. As the organization grew, it established itself as a community-based volunteer organization dedicated to fighting the AIDS epidemic. (Courtesy Scott Stites.)

Members of the Royal Court of the Golden Spike Empire crowned Scott Stites as Emperor X in 1986. As the 10th reigning emperor during the early years of the AIDS epidemic, Stites focused on activism to raise money for people with AIDS. The first fundraiser brought together many of the gay and lesbian groups in Utah and raised $10,000. Stites also created AIDS Awareness Week in Utah. (Courtesy Scott Stites.)

The Royal Court of the Golden Spike Empire crowned Mother Bob Empress X in 1986. She worked with Emperor Scott Stites to raise money and awareness for people with AIDS in Utah. As empress, Mother Bob announced that $1 from the sale of each coronation ticket would be donated to charity. In 1986, the money raised went to AIDS Project Utah. (Courtesy Scott Stites.)

AIDS AWARENESS WEEK

is proudly being sponsored by

AIDS PROJECT UTAH
AFFIRMATION
DIGNITY
GOLDEN SPIKE GAY RODEO ASSOCIATION
KNIGHTS OF MALTA
LESBIAN AND GAY STUDENT UNION
METROPOLITAN COMMUNITY CHURCH
ROYAL COURT OF THE GOLDEN SPIKE EMPIRE
SALT LAKE AIDS FOUNDATION
UTAH AIDS FOUNDATION
UTAH COMMUNITY CENTER AND CLINIC
WASATCH LEATHERMEN'S CLUB
BACKSTREET
BLUE HORIZON
DEER HUNTER
JOURNAL
PUSS AND BOOTS
RADIO CITY
SUN TAVERN
THREE ACES

October 5th thru 12th

This flyer created by the Royal Court of the Golden Spike Empire during the first AIDS Awareness Week lists AIDS organizations such as AIDS Project Utah and the Salt Lake AIDS Foundation, religious groups like MCC, Affirmation, and Dignity (a support group for gay Catholics), and bars such as the Sun Tavern, Puss and Boots, the Deer Hunter, as well as other organizations that collaborated to raise over $10,000 for people with AIDS in 1986. (Courtesy Scott Stites.)

Michael Spence performed as Tracey Ross, Princess Royal VI in the Royal Court of the Golden Spike Empire. Spence passed away from complications related to AIDS and was honored in an AIDS Memorial Quilt panel made by community activist Ben Williams in 1988. (Courtesy Scott Stites.)

The Lovebirds, a drag act based on girl groups from the 1960s, performed around Salt Lake City in the 1980s. The ladies performed at the Wasatch Leathermen's annual motorcycle run and were the first drag act to perform at Symphony Hall, appearing alongside Roseanne Barr and Louie Anderson. They are pictured here at Pride Day in 1986 at Sunnyside Park. (Courtesy Curtis Jensen.)

When Bruce Barton returned to Salt Lake City in the early 1980s, he became the pastor for the Metropolitan Community Church. The small congregation met at the Unitarian church until Barton found a new location. Under Barton, the congregation once again began to grow in membership, so the church renamed itself the Resurrection Metropolitan Community Church. He is pictured here with Marlene, a member of the Lovebirds. (Courtesy Curtis Jensen.)

Becky Moss expanded the title of the KRCL radio show from *Concerning Gays* to *Concerning Gays and Lesbians* when she became cohost. Throughout the 1980s, the radio show addressed issues pertaining to the community. Moss dedicated at least one episode a month to raising awareness about AIDS. She has been a longtime activist in the LGBT community in Utah. Moss is pictured here filing paperwork to run for mayor of Millcreek City in 2016. (Courtesy Becky Moss.)

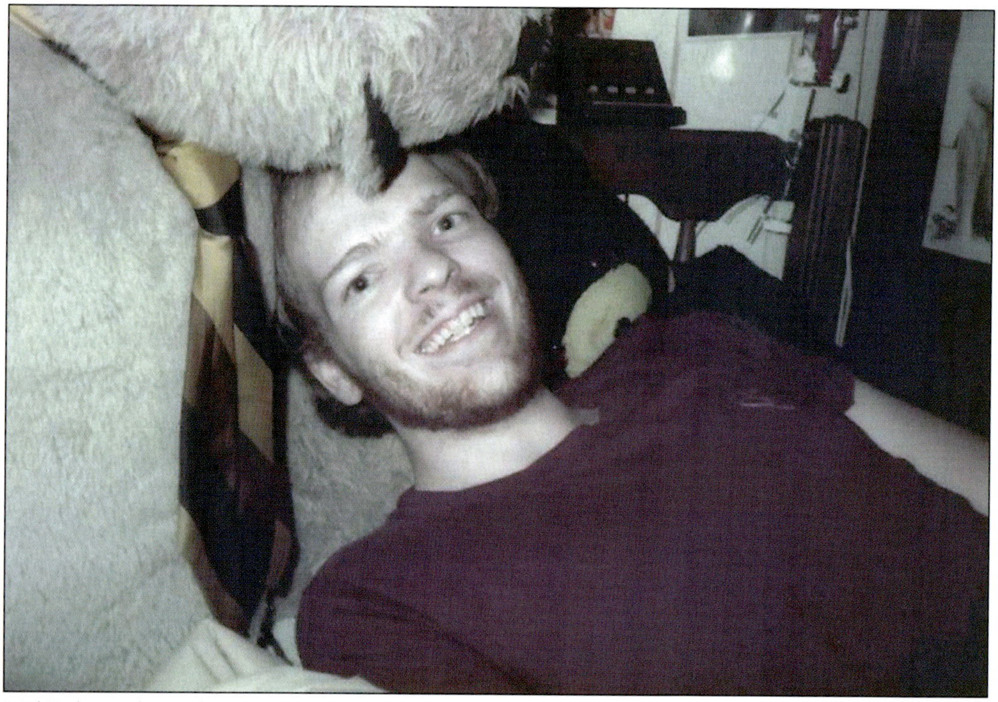

Mel Baker cohosted the weekly radio show *Concerning Gays and Lesbians* with Becky Moss from approximately 1983 to 1987 on KRCL. Baker served on the national planning committee for the 1987 March on Washington, and the Gay and Lesbian Community Council raised funds to send Baker as a representative of Utah to the march. (Courtesy Wess Mongo Jolley.)

Carol Lynn Pearson is a well-known Mormon poet, playwright, and author. She published a memoir in 1986 titled *Goodbye, I Love You* detailing her marriage to a gay man, their divorce, and his death from AIDS in 1984. For decades, she has been a gentle but firm voice for LGBT rights within Mormonism and has helped thousands of people struggling with faith and sexuality. (Courtesy Utah Stonewall Historical Society.)

Ben Barr played an important role as a major fundraiser and AIDS educator during the 1980s. He served as the executive director of AIDS Project Utah and the Salt Lake AIDS Foundation and helped raise money to bring the Names Project AIDS Memorial Quilt to the state in 1989. He received the Dr. Kristen Ries Award in 1993 for his work fighting AIDS and received a Lifetime Achievement Award from Utah Pride in 2011. His work has had a lasting impact on the LGBT community in Utah. (Courtesy University of Utah.)

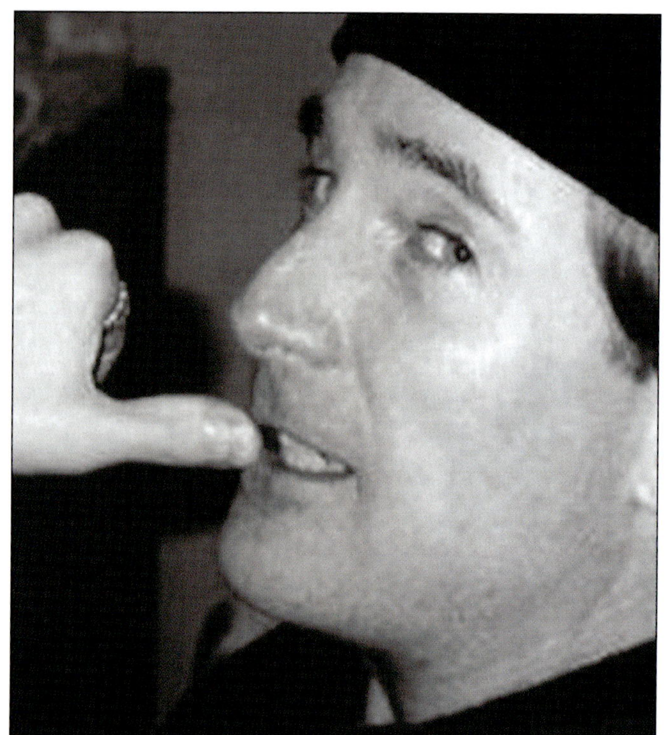

David K. Nelson, a longtime gay rights activist in Utah, played a large role in shaping the political climate of Utah. He served as vice president of the Lesbian and Gay Student Union at the University of Utah, helped found Gay Community, Inc., in 1985, served as copublisher of the *Community Reporter*, and ran for city council as an openly gay man that same year. He helped found the Gay and Lesbian Community Council of Utah in 1986, founded Gay and Lesbian Utah Democrats in 1990, and wrote the first nondiscrimination ordinance for Salt Lake County that passed in 1992. (Courtesy Utah Stonewall Historical Society.)

Members of Affirmation: Gay and Lesbian Mormons participated in the Second National March on Washington for Lesbian and Gay Rights in October 1987. Their presence as lesbian, gay, bisexual, and transgender people of faith disrupts the idea that gender or sexual minority identities and religious identities are incompatible. (Courtesy Affirmation.)

Gordon Ray Church, a gay man from Fillmore, Utah, met Michael Archuleta and Lance Wood in November 1988 at a convenience store in Cedar City. The three men drove up Cedar Canyon, where Archuleta and Wood tortured and then murdered Church in what is one of the most vicious crimes in Utah history. Archuleta received the death penalty, while Wood received life in prison. (Courtesy Chad Anderson.)

The Desert & Mountain States Lesbian and Gay Conference held its fifth annual conference in Salt Lake City in May 1989. More than 150 activists from Nevada, Utah, Colorado, Arizona, New Mexico, and Wyoming gathered for a three-day conference with the theme "Forging Our Destiny." The conference had 30 workshops covering topics such as "Lesbian Leadership," "Internalized Homophobia: From Despair to Hope," and "Lesbian and Gay Youth." (Courtesy University of Utah.)

Becky Moorman and Alice Hart, owners of the Rhino Nest bookstore, began publishing the *Bridge*, which focused on lesbian and gay arts and entertainment, in 1990. By then, the phrase "lesbian and gay," as opposed to just the word *gay*, was used to mark gender distinctions between people within the community, as evidenced by this publication. (Courtesy University of Utah.)

In February 1991, Connell O'Donovan, Curtis Jensen, and Melanie Bailey formed Queer Nation Utah with the stated purpose of promoting queer visibility. Queer Nation Utah demonstrated near Temple Square during the April 1991 LDS General Conference to fight back against the growing homophobia espoused by church leaders. They chanted, "Two, four, six, eight, how do you know your bishop's straight?" and "We're here, we're queer, we're fabulous, get used to us." (Courtesy Curtis Jensen.)

Toni Palmer carries the sign "Stop Queer Bashing" at the protest in 1991. The use of the word *queer* in Utah and nationally signaled a shift in language deployed by people who rejected the terms *gay* and *lesbian* because the words were gendered, classed, and raced. With *queer*, people unified around a shared dissent that altered categorical boundaries. (Courtesy Curtis Jensen.)

From 1991 to 1992, Prof. Henry Abelove spent a year on sabbatical in Salt Lake City, where he joined Queer Nation Utah as a full participant, not as a researcher. As a scholar, he helped provide the intellectual framework and discourse that guided the emergent queer radical movement in Utah. After retiring from Wesleyan University in 2011, he returned to teach one more semester in the first endowed faculty position for LGBTQ studies at Harvard. (Courtesy Henry Abelove.)

As part of the Suburban Homosexual Outreach Program (S.H.O.P.), members of Queer Nation Utah went into shopping malls to promote queer visibility by festooning themselves in queer paraphernalia, including stickers with the words *fag*, *dyke*, and *queer*. Doing so marked them as unashamed of their sexuality. They took this "family portrait" in 1991. (Courtesy Curtis Jensen.)

Connell "Rocky" O'Donovan organized Utah's first Gay and Lesbian Pride March in 1990 and the second in 1991. The march ended at the Salt Lake City and County Building, where this photograph was taken. In 1991, organizers of the annual Pride Day moved the festival to the fairgrounds in Murray. During these years, the march and festival were held on different days. (Courtesy Connell O'Donovan.)

On June 27, 1991, the gay and lesbian community marched through Salt Lake City escorted by more than a dozen police officers. On this day, a group of about 15 neo-Nazis carrying signs and flags with swastikas gathered on the steps of the Salt Lake City and County Building, where the march ended. Those who had participated turned their backs on the neo-Nazis but had to endure slurs shouted at them, like "out of the closet and into the grave" and "thank God for AIDS." No physical confrontations occurred. (Courtesy Connell O'Donovan.)

March organizer Connell "Rocky" O'Donovan addressed the crowd through a megaphone. He told the crowd to remain calm, to ignore the Nazi presence, and to celebrate and take pride in who they were as gay and lesbian people. (Courtesy Connell O'Donovan.)

Members of Queer Nation Utah handed out balloons during the Days of '47 Parade in July 1991. The balloons read "Utah—a great place for Queers," a slogan that parodied the state's unpopular tourist slogan, "Utah—a pretty, great state." (Courtesy Curtis Jensen.)

About three dozen gay rights activists observed the fourth National Coming Out Day in October 1991 by carrying placards and rainbow flags while marching around the US Federal Building at 125 South State Street. Later that evening, the Utah Stonewall Center hosted a reception. (Courtesy Curtis Jensen.)

Four

Political Incorporation and Legal Advancements 1992–2006

By the early 1990s, gays and lesbians had expanded into the political realm. David K. Nelson in 1990 founded Gay and Lesbian Utah Democrats, which helped elect Democrats to the Salt Lake County Commission, lobbied for the successful passage of the state's first nondiscrimination ordinance at the county level, and in 1992 fought for a nondiscrimination clause to the Utah Democratic Party platform that included "sexual orientation" and forbade discrimination in party affairs. Michael Aaron led the Anti-Violence Campaign by gathering statistics to document violence towards gays and lesbians in Utah and lobbied for passage of a hate crimes bill. Peggy Tingey and Cindy Kidd sued the state in 1993 to overturn a 1987 law that made marriages of any person with AIDS "null and void." Federal judge Aldon Anderson ruled in their favor and overturned the law. Shortly after the ruling, Tingey and Kidd passed away due to complication from AIDS.

In late 1995, Kelli Peterson, a 17-year-old student from East High School, formed the first Gay Straight Alliance (GSA) in Utah. The club's formation caused an outcry that involved national conservative leaders, the state legislature, and the local school board, which eventually voted 4-3 to ban all extracurricular clubs rather than approve the GSA as required by the Federal Equal Access Act of 1984, a bill sponsored by Utah senator Orrin Hatch. Clayton Vetter, a member of the Gay, Lesbian, and Straight Teachers Network, came out as gay at a press conference, making him the first public schoolteacher in the state to publicly acknowledge his sexual orientation.

Kathy Worthington published the *Womyn's Community Newsletter* for four years beginning in 1991. She also won an important battle against her employer, the United States Postal Service, when she was granted unpaid leave in 1997 to care for her partner, Sara Hamblin, who was undergoing chemotherapy. The next year, Jackie Biskupski ran for the Utah House of Representatives as an openly gay candidate. She won her election in 1998 and served her District 30 constituents for 13 years.

The ACLU became more involved in fighting for gay and lesbian rights in Utah during the 1990s. The ACLU represented Wendy Weaver, a teacher from Spanish Fork High School who had been threatened with job loss if she talked about her sexuality on or off campus. Her lawsuit, *Weaver v. Nebo School District*, alleged the school district had violated her rights to free expression, privacy, and equal protection. In a landmark ruling that was hailed as one of the best decisions for LGBT teachers in the country, Judge Bruce Jenkins of the US District Court for the District of Utah ruled in favor of Weaver in 1998.

Utah Democratic Party delegates appointed Scott McCoy to a vacant senate seat in 2005, making McCoy the first openly gay man to serve in the state senate. In 2006, he won reelection, while Christine A. Johnson won her election to the Utah House of Representatives, making her the third openly gay member of the legislature. Jennifer Lee Jackson ran as the first transgender woman in a primary for a seat in the state senate, but she lost the primary.

The Anti-Violence Project documented 273 violent attacks against gays and lesbians in 1990. Rep. Frank Pignanelli sponsored two hate crime bills in 1992 that would have included sexual orientation as a protected class. Joy Beech of Families Alert and other conservatives strongly opposed the bill. When the legislature passed a bill that did not include language protecting sexual orientation, members of the gay and lesbian community protested at the capitol. (Courtesy Curtis Jensen.)

Michael Aaron has worked as a gay rights activist in Utah for decades. He was a member of the Lesbian and Gay Student Union (LGSU) at the University of Utah, helped organize the first Pride Week in Utah, published the *Community Reporter* and *Triangle* magazine from 1985 to 1988, attended the Marches on Washington in 1987 and 1993, helped organize the Anti-Violence Project, and has held leadership positions in the Salt Lake Men's Choir, Utah Stonewall Center, Gay and Lesbian Community Council, and many other organizations. Since 2004, he has published *QSalt Lake*. (Courtesy Utah Stonewall Historical Society.)

With grant money secured by Charlene Orchard, the first Utah Stonewall Center opened at 450 South 900 East on June 1, 1991. As the center grew, it relocated in 1993 to 770 South 300 West, pictured here. Volunteers staffed the center, which served as a meeting place for a variety of groups, including the Utah Stonewall Historical Society, Affirmation, Gay and Lesbian Community Council, and youth groups. Conflicts within the board of directors and financial struggles led to the center's closure on October 1, 1997. (Courtesy Utah Stonewall Historical Society.)

The political career of Randy Horiuchi (left) spanned many years in Utah. He served on the Salt Lake County Commission and Salt Lake County Council. Although he was not gay, he sponsored the first nondiscrimination ordinance in the state that included protections for sexual orientation at the county level in 1992. He fought for democratic reforms, mentored future leaders, and was beloved by many in Salt Lake City. He passed away in 2015 at the age of 61. (Courtesy Rob Miller.)

Antonia De La Guerra organized the third Salt Lake Pride March, held on June 24, 1992. About 250 people gathered at the capitol before marching to the Salt Lake City and County Building. Speakers built on the theme "power equals pride" and urged those in attendance to get involved in politics. Greg Garcia of Wasatch Leathermen motorcycle club told the press, "We have the pride to overcome any prejudice." (Courtesy Curtis Jensen.)

Dale Sorenson was a member of Utah Gay and Lesbian Youth and LGSU and volunteered for the Utah AIDS Foundation. He served as an executive officer for the Gay and Lesbian Utah Democrats from 1990 to 1992, then as executive director from 1992 to 1994. He helped pass the first nondiscrimination ordinance in the state, testified before the legislature about hate crimes, and organized Pride Day and National Coming Out Day in Utah. (Courtesy University of Utah.)

Ben Williams converted to the LDS Church and moved to Utah to attend BYU in the early 1970s. He struggled to reconcile his adopted religion with his sexuality. After years of trying to change his sexual orientation, he came out as gay in 1986 and got divorced. He became active in the local gay community by starting social and political groups, including Unconditional Support and the Utah Stonewall Center. Williams has received many awards for his work as an activist and historian of Utah's LGBT community. (Courtesy Utah Stonewall Historical Society.)

Members of the Gay and Lesbian Alliance at Utah State University in Logan rode on a float at the 1992 Homecoming Parade, marking the first time a gay-themed float appeared in a parade in Utah. People complained to the university about the use of the word *homo* on a sign that read "homo-coming '92." (Courtesy Courtney Moser.)

In 1993, AIDS activist Peggy Tingey—pictured here with her husband, Bill, daughter, Amanda Moss, and son, Chance—learned that a 1987 state law made her marriage "null and void" because she was HIV-positive at the time she married in 1989. In July 1993, Tingey, along with Cindy Kidd, another heterosexual, married woman with HIV, sued the state in *T.E.P., et al. v. Leavitt, et al.* In September 1993, a federal judge overturned the law. Due to complications from AIDS, Tingey and Chance, who was born HIV-positive, both passed away shortly after the lawsuit ended. (Courtesy Becky Moss.)

The *Pillar* added the word *bisexual* to its selling line in the early 1990s. The acronym GLB had begun to form, but the *T* had not yet come into widespread use. In this issue from 1994, the cover story focuses on two attorneys from the ACLU of Utah: Utah native Kate Kendall (left), who today is executive director for the National Center for Lesbian Rights, and Carole Gnade, who today is executive director for the Utah Pride Center. (Courtesy Duane Jennings.)

While a senior at East High School in 1996, Kelli Peterson started the first Gay Straight Alliance in the state, for which she and the club became the center of a national debate about the purpose and legality of such clubs. The school board voted to remove all extracurricular clubs from campus rather than allow the GSA. The ACLU challenged the decision. After several years of litigation, the Salt Lake City School Board reversed its decision in October 2000. Filmmakers featured Peterson and the controversy about the GSA in a PBS documentary, *Out of the Past*, in 1998. (Courtesy Don Romesburg.)

Jacob Orozco, a student at East High, wraps his arms around Kelli Peterson during filming for the documentary. Orozco had been an active member of the GSA and was supposed to be the next president, but he committed suicide in 1997, when he was 17. Filmmakers Jeff Dupre and Eliza Byard mourned his death in an e-mail to Lambda Legal in which they noted the pain and loneliness faced by LGBT youth at the hands of a homophobic culture. (Courtesy Don Romesburg.)

During the debate about the Gay Straight Alliance, the Utah Human Rights Coalition called a press conference in February 1996 to announce the formation of the Utah chapter of the Gay, Lesbian, and Straight Teachers Network. At this event, Clayton Vetter, a well-respected teacher and debate coach at Skyline High School who had received awards and recognition for his teaching, came out as gay, risking his career to do so. (Courtesy Clayton Vetter.)

March 21-23, 1997
Salt Lake City, Utah
Downtown Holiday Inn

A Weekend of Strategizing, Planning, and Fun for Everyone who Wants to See Our Schools Become Places Where All People are Respected.

People of Color Intensive
Led by GLSTN Program Associate Deidre Cuffee-Gray, this workshop will explore the particular demands faced by people of color doing anti-homophobia work. Participation is limited to people of color, who may come from any occupational background or sexual identity group.

FRIDAY EVENING OPENING RECEPTION

Join your friends (both old ones and ones you haven't met yet!) at an informal reception at the Holiday Inn to kick-off the conference week-end. Featured speakers will include Kelli Peterson, the student founder of the East High School Gay-Straight Alliance, Clayton Vetter, the first openly gay public school teacher in Utah history, and GLSTN Executive Director Kevin Jennings.

SATURDAY MARCH 22 Conference Opens

Saturday Keynote Address: Urvashi Vaid
Veteran activist Urvashi Vaid (author of *Virtual Equality*) will share her thoughts on the past, present, and future of our movement. Drawing on her career as an attorney, journalist, and past Executive Director of the National Gay and Lesbian Task Force, Urvashi will help us think about how to meet the challenges we face as we move ahead with our work

Workshops Sessions: All Day Saturday and Sunday Morning
Participants can choose among over 40 workshops designed to give them concrete skills to use in their work in ending homophobia in their community's schools. Topics will speak to the needs of both those inside and outside of schools, and will include such diverse subjects as "Starting Gay-Straight Alliances," "Impacting your Community's School Board Elections," and "Legal Issues for Teachers."

SUNDAY MARCH 23

Sunday Celebration Brunch with comic Suzanne Westenhoefer
The conference will close with a celebratory brunch with nationally-known comic Suzanne Westenhoefer. Known for her appearances on HBO and other venues, Suzanne will share her experiences as not only a comedian but also an educator who does special outreach through performances for high school audiences in the cities where she tours. The brunch will also feature presentation of GLSTN's annual "Pathfinder Awards" to those who have made a special contribution to the fight to create schools where all people are respected.

In response to the legislature's hostility towards the Gay Straight Alliance and the school board's vote to ban all extracurricular clubs, the Gay, Lesbian, and Straight Teachers Network (later the Gay, Lesbian, Straight Education Network, or GLSEN) held its first national conference in Salt Lake City in March 1997. Kelli Peterson and Clayton Vetter received awards. (Courtesy Clayton Vetter.)

Voters of District 30 supported Jackie Biskupski for the Utah House of Representatives in 1998, making her the first openly gay person elected to the state legislature. Because of her sexuality, she faced fierce opposition from antigay organizations in Utah, including the ultraconservative Eagle Forum. Biskupski won the election in 1998 and subsequent reelections until she resigned in 2011. She is pictured here in the Utah Pride Parade in 1999. (Courtesy Rob Schlittler, *Out and Elected in the USA: 1974–2004*, outhistory.org.)

The Lesbian and Gay Chorus performed in the 1990s at Pride Day, memorial services, conferences, community events, and at the First Baptist Church during the holidays. Under the direction of Meloni Gunderson, the chorus often sang music written by lesbian and gay composers. (Courtesy Renee Rinaldi.)

Scott McCoy (second from left) served as executive director for the Don't Amend Alliance, a group against passage of a constitutional amendment banning recognition of same-sex marriage in Utah. The campaign worked to educate voters about Amendment 3 and how it would hurt the lives of friends, families, and neighbors. The campaign raised a substantial amount of money and had strong support, but Amendment 3 passed on November 2, 2004, with 66 percent of the vote. (Courtesy Scott McCoy.)

Krystal Etsitty began working for Utah Transit Authority in 2001 but was fired in 2002 after her employers learned she was transgender. In *Etsitty v. Utah Transit Authority*, her attorneys argued that Title VII of the Civil Rights Act protected transgender citizens from discrimination, but the judge disagreed. In 2007, the US Court of Appeals for the Tenth Circuit affirmed the district court's decision in favor of the transit authority. (Courtesy Krystal Etsitty.)

Gov. John Huntsman Jr. swore the first openly gay Utah state senator, Scott McCoy, into office in 2005. As a member of the senate, McCoy, along with three other Democrats in the legislature, sponsored the 2009 Common Ground Initiative, a set of five bills aimed at enhancing legal protections for LGBT Utahns. The initiative arose in response to statements from LDS Church leadership that they did not oppose some rights for LGBT people. At that time, the initiative was the most expansive legislative push for gay rights in the state, but none of the bills made it out of committee. (Courtesy Scott McCoy.)

In 2005, Elizabeth "Beano" Solomon applied for three vanity license plates—including one that read, "GAYSROK"—to show support for her gay daughter and gay friends. The Utah Motor Vehicles Division refused the application, saying the plates would be "offensive to good taste and decency, relate to sexual functions and express superiority of a gender." Solomon appealed the decision, and the tax commission overturned the ruling. (Courtesy Beano Solomon.)

In 2006, Jennifer Lee Jackson ran in the Salt Lake County Democratic primary for a seat in the state senate against former state representative Trisha Beck. Jackson lost to Beck but received wide media coverage as the first transgender person to run in a primary election in Utah. (Courtesy Michael Aaron.)

Voters elected Christine Johnson to the Utah House of Representatives for District 25 in 2006 with 75 percent of the vote. She joined Jackie Biskupski and Scott McCoy as the third LGBT person elected to the legislature. Prior to the election, she had been vice-chair of the Stonewall Democrats and a board member of Equality Utah. She did not seek reelection in 2010; instead, she took a position as the executive director of South Carolina Equality. (Courtesy Christine Johnson.)

Five

Marriage Equality, Proposition 8, and Its Aftermath 2007–2010

In 2004, Rep. LaVar Christensen (R-Draper) authored an amendment to the Utah state constitution that defined marriage as a union exclusively between one man and one woman, even though Utah law had prohibited same-sex marriage since 1977. The Don't Amend Alliance formed to fight what became known as Amendment 3, but voters in Utah passed the measure in November 2004 by 66 percent of the vote.

A watershed moment for LGBT rights came in 2008, when the LDS Church vigorously fought marriage equality in California. In an attempt to rescind the right to marriage that had become legal in California earlier that year, opponents of marriage equality added Proposition 8 to the ballot. The First Presidency of the LDS Church sent a letter to local leaders to be read in church meetings that asked members of the church to do all they could to support passage of Proposition 8 by donating "means and time." The campaign turned divisive and painful to many families around the country. News outlets, church meetings, religious leaders, and gay rights organizations argued bitterly over questions of religious intrusion, faith, sexuality, and rights for LGBT people as citizens. Shock and outrage spread nationwide when Proposition 8 passed with 52 percent of the vote in 2008. In Utah, Jacob Whipple organized a demonstration that drew thousands of people and received extensive media coverage as crowds marched through the streets of downtown Salt Lake City and around Temple Square. Meanwhile, the legal framework had been put into motion that would ultimately push the question of same-sex marriage before the Supreme Court.

During the years after Proposition 8, the LGBT community held many rallies and marches in support of LGBT rights. Rep. Christine Johnson introduced a bill to protect LGBT people from employment and housing discrimination in 2008, but the bill did not make it out of committee. In 2009, legislators working with Equality Utah proposed the Common Ground Initiative to work towards securing rights for LGBT Utahns. The LDS Church supported a citywide nondiscrimination bill passed by the city council that gave housing and employment protections to LGBT people, yet attacks on LGBT people by the state legislature continued. No pro-LGBT bills passed, but Equality Utah recognized the advances being made at the 2010 Equality Utah Allies dinner with the theme "Gaining Ground."

Three Mormon mothers of gay children, Millie Watts, Linda Barney, and Kathryn Steffensen, organized an anti–Prop 8 vigil at Library Square on November 2, 2008. The mothers spoke, often through tears, about the pain and division the LDS Church caused by supporting the anti-marriage amendment. After the vigil, the crowd walked around the block with candles and "No on 8" signs. (Courtesy David Daniels.)

When Proposition 8 passed, an estimated 3,500 people gathered in downtown Salt Lake City to protest the LDS Church's political involvement in California. The organization Protect Marriage estimated that LDS church members contributed nearly half of the $40 million raised for the measure. In 2010, the California Fair Political Practices Commission fined the LDS Church for violating the state's political contributions law for failing to report on time the contributions made by the church. (Courtesy David Daniels.)

The anti–Proposition 8 crowd gathered in City Creek Park with signs and flags. After the speeches, people marched along North Temple past the LDS Church Office Building, where they chanted, "What do we want? Equality. When do we want it? Now!" LGBT people and allies also marched around LDS sites in California and Arizona. (Courtesy David Daniels.)

After Proposition 8 passed, Jacob Whipple (right) organized a demonstration that drew thousands and dominated news coverage. He spoke to the crowd along with the three LGBT members of the legislature and the former mayor of Salt Lake City, Rocky Anderson (left). Whipple said, "We need to make it known that we are hurt; we need to make it known that we will stand up for our rights." (Courtesy David Daniels.)

The Sutherland Institute invited members of Equality Utah to debate the Common Ground Initiative in February 2009 at the University of Utah law school. From left to right are Sutherland president Paul Mero, board member Rep. LaVar Christensen, field education director for the BYU College of Family Shirley Cox, and Center for Family and Society director Bill Duncan. In his opening remarks, Mero argued, "your version of marriage and family are an illusion. . . . You play house as only a dysfunctional household structure could allow." (Courtesy David Daniels.)

The Equality Utah team included, from left to right, law professor and Equality Utah board member Cliff Rosky, psychologist Lee Beckstead, attorney and Utah state senator Scott McCoy, and Equality Utah manager of public policy and attorney Will Carlson. Carlson argued that the Common Ground Initiative provided LGBT people with inheritance rights as well as protections from housing and job discrimination. The legislature did not pass the initiative. (Courtesy David Daniels.)

In May 2009, the California Supreme Court upheld Proposition 8 but also ruled that the 18,000 same-sex couples who married before the vote would continue to have their marriages recognized by the state. The LGBT community and allies gathered at the Utah State Capitol to stand in solidarity and vowed to keep fighting for marriage equality. (Courtesy David Daniels.)

On October 11, 2009, thousands of LGBT people marched from the White House to the Capitol calling for protections for LGBT people in civil law during the National Equality March. About 100 members of the community in Utah who could not travel to Washington met at the Pride Center at 355 North 300 West and marched several blocks to Club Sound, where they watched a live broadcast of the events in Washington. (Courtesy David Daniels.)

Radio City Lounge, at 147 South State Street, remained a part of the downtown Salt Lake City community for 61 years. By the mid-1990s, it had evolved into a gay bar, and people continued to patronize the location (pictured here a few weeks before demolition) until it met the wrecking ball in 2009. (Courtesy Gaytravel.about.com.)

Utahns on both sides of the marriage equality debate watched closely as the rancorous legal proceedings in California moved up to the federal level. On August 4, 2010, when federal judge Vaughn Walker overturned Proposition 8, several hundred people gathered again at the Utah State Capitol to celebrate the victory. (Courtesy David Daniels.)

The return of marriage equality in California did not bring marriage equality to the nation, but activists and legal experts expected the issue to go before the Supreme Court. Eric Ethington-Boden organized a rally and march. He told the press, "We do a lot of protests in Utah. Utah is a state that you have to fight tooth and nail for them to recognize you as a human being. Thank goodness in this instance common decency and law triumphed over religious opinion." (Courtesy David Daniels.)

Activist Isaac Higham addressed the estimated 600 people at the rally, saying that while marriage equality was winning in the courts, the community could not become complacent. Other issues, such as passage of nondiscrimination laws, LGBT immigration reform, and repeal of Don't Ask Don't Tell were topics still facing the LGBT community. (Courtesy David Daniels.)

In 2008, actor Charles Lynn Frost cocreated and played the character Sister Dottie S. Dixon, a Mormon housewife with a gay son. Sister Dottie's humor comes through in her thick Utah County accent and malapropisms. Her wisdom and love resonated with the LGBT community for her refusal to choose her religion over her son. She has appeared in two stage productions, hosts fundraisers, and also makes appearances at community events and rallies. (Courtesy David Daniels.)

Chris Buttars fought against LGBT rights while serving in the state senate from 2001 to 2011. He cosponsored Amendment 3, introduced legislation to ban Gay Straight Alliances, and introduced legislation designed to prevent cities or counties from creating domestic partner registries. Buttars referred to Utah state senator Scott McCoy as "the gay" and said that gays and lesbians were "the greatest threat to America going down." He was eventually removed as chairman of the Senate Judicial Standing Committee. (Courtesy David Daniels.)

Gayle Ruzika is a conservative political activist. As president of the Utah Eagle Forum, she and the organization opposed the formation of Gay Straight Alliances for LGBT students, fought efforts to pass a nondiscrimination bill, fought against the Common Ground Initiative, fought against sex education, and helped pass Utah's ban on marriage equality. Ruzika is not an elected official but is considered one of the most influential people in Utah politics. (Courtesy David Daniels.)

Brandi Balken, a lifelong Utahn, became executive director of Equality Utah in 2009 in a volatile political atmosphere. Under her leadership, Equality Utah passed 10 LGBT-friendly city ordinances in 2010, forged relationships with politicians and other community leaders, and helped grow the Allies Award dinner to fill the largest ballroom in the state. She stepped down in 2014 to take a position with the Gill Foundation and is remembered as one of the finest and most effective leaders in Utah. (Courtesy David Daniels.)

Equality Utah, Utah Pride Center, and the First Unitarian Church of Salt Lake City organized the Joyful Sound for Common Ground rally at the capitol in 2010. Brandi Balken said, "We feel that now is the perfect time to stand together and celebrate the many things we, as residents of Utah, agree on." Academy Award winner Dustin Lance Black also spoke at the event. (Courtesy David Daniels.)

Filmmaker Reed Cowan (center) premiered his film *8: The Mormon Proposition* at the Sundance Film Festival in 2010. The documentary explores the role of the LDS Church in passing Proposition 8 and the effects of family rejection on LGBT youth. He is pictured here along with Utah native Kate Kendall, executive director of the National Center for Lesbian Rights, and screenwriter Dustin Lance Black discussing the film. (Courtesy David Daniels.)

For many, the Proposition 8 debate highlighted the incompatibility between LGBT people and people of faith, but this position ignores the multiple religious denominations that support and honor LGBT people. The Community of Christ (pictured here), formerly known as the Re-organized Church of Jesus Christ of Latter-day Saints, a cousin denomination to the LDS Church, recognizes same-sex marriage and ordains LGBT members to the priesthood. (Author's collection.)

The First Baptist Church at 800 South and 1300 East has long been a supporter of the LGBT community. In the mid-1990s, it rented space to the Lesbian and Gay Chorus to perform, and it also rents space to the Matrons of Mayhem to host the monthly drag bingo. The church has also hosted the annual Pride Interfaith Service. (Courtesy David Daniels.)

In 1970, the Unitarian Universalist Association General Assembly passed a resolution that has become the foundation for the denomination's long-standing affirmation of LGBT people. During the AIDS epidemic, the Unitarians in Salt Lake City opened their doors for support groups to host meetings for people with AIDS. In 1990, Utah-based Unitarian minister Barbara Hamilton-Holway officiated marriage ceremonies between same-sex couples, although the state did not recognize the unions as legal. (Author's collection.)

St. Paul's Episcopal Church in Salt Lake City has long accepted LGBT people into the congregation. In the 1980s, the church helped care for people with AIDS by providing housing and food. In 2003, the Episcopal Church USA ordained Gene Robinson, an openly gay prelate, as bishop of New Hampshire. In 2015, the General Convention of the Episcopal Church was held in Salt Lake City, where delegates voted to embrace marriage equality. (Author's collection.)

Six

A Queer New World 2011–2016

Utah felt the effects of the Supreme Court's decision regarding same-sex marriage in 2013 after the decisions in the Defense of Marriage Act (*United States v. Windsor*) and Proposition 8 (*Hollingsworth v. Perry*) cases. Mark Lawrence, executive director of the nonprofit Restore Our Humanity, devised a legal case to challenge Amendment 3 in Utah. He hired attorneys from the firm Magleby Cataxinos & Greenwood to represent three couples who challenged the law when they filed *Kitchen v. Herbert* on March 25, 2013. Utah made history on December 20, 2013, when federal judge Robert Shelby ruled in favor of the plaintiffs and did not stay his decision, making Utah the 18th state (plus the District of Columbia) with marriage equality. Less than an hour after the ruling, same-sex couples began to legally marry in Utah until the Supreme Court stayed Judge Shelby's decision on January 6, 2014. Attorneys for the state filed appeals that they argued before the Tenth Circuit on April 10, 2014, and on October 6, 2014, the Supreme Court refused to hear the state's appeal, effectively returning marriage equality to Utah and the states included in the Tenth Circuit.

Since then, the LGBT community has had a series of other successes and setbacks. After eight years, the legislature passed a nondiscrimination bill in 2015 that added employment and housing protections for LGBT people. The Damn These Heels LGBT Film Festival, hosted by the Utah Film Center, continued to expand. Groups such as the Trans Education Alliance and Trans-Action became more visible, as did transgender activists such as Gabriel Glissmeyer, Grayson Moore, and Candice Metzler. In 2015, students at the Salt Lake School for the Performing Arts elected a transgender woman, Maka Brown, as homecoming queen and a gay man, Jasper Clayton, as prom king. Jackie Biskupski won her campaign for mayor of Salt Lake City, making her the second female and the first LGBT person to serve in that capacity. Voters elected Stan Penfold, an openly gay man and executive director of the Utah AIDS Foundation, to the Salt Lake City Council in 2010 then elected Derek Kitchen, the second openly gay man, to the city council in 2015. The following year, the Volunteers of America opened a 20,000-square-foot resource center that provides overnight shelter for homeless teens, many of whom identify as LGBT, and the city council voted unanimously in favor of renaming a prominent downtown street Harvey Milk Boulevard. Later that year, Dexter Thomas, a transgender man from Salt Lake City, won PETA's "Sexiest Vegan Next Door" award and the Utah Democratic Party made history by nominating Misty K. Snow as the first transgender nominee from a major party to run for a US Senate seat.

Meanwhile, an attempt to update the state's Hate Crime law failed, groups promoting conversion therapy continue to operate in Utah, the LDS Church adopted more aggressive anti-LGBT policies, and suicide among youth, many of whom identify as LGBT, continues to be the leading cause of death for young people in the state. Despite these setbacks and tragedies, the LGBT community in Utah continues to thrive as it works towards justice and equality for all in a queer new world.

Roseanne Barr grew up in Utah and has two gay siblings. Her sharp wit mixed with a fiery brand of feminism and fearlessness led to a successful career as a stand-up comic, but it was her television program that made her a household name. Her critically acclaimed show *Roseanne* included openly gay characters and showed a same-sex kiss as well as a same-sex wedding in the 1990s. During the 1980s, she did a series of benefits for AIDS causes in Utah. Utah Pride recognized her as the grand marshal in 2011. (Courtesy David Daniels.)

Jim Dabakis cofounded the Utah Pride Center and Equality Utah. In July 2011, he was elected chair of the Utah Democratic Party, and Democratic delegates appointed him to the Utah Senate in December 2012, making him the second openly gay man to serve in the senate and the fourth openly gay person to serve in the Utah State Legislature. He won reelection in 2014. After Gov. Gary Herbert swore him into office, he presented the pen used to sign the paperwork to Stephen Justesen, Dabakis's partner and now husband. (Courtesy Stephen Justesen.)

Connie A. Anast-Inman, then serving as executive director of Transgender Education Advocates (TEA) of Utah, spoke about "The Unknown, Missing & Unnamed" at the 14th Annual International Transgender Day of Remembrance in November 2012 at the First United Methodist Church. She reminded the audience that ignorance and hatred led to violence and death of transgender citizens and that the community had a responsibility to strive every day for equality, dignity, and respect for all members of society. (Courtesy TEA of Utah.)

Dominique Storni is a well-known activist within the LGBT community. She speaks at rallies, participates in political demonstrations, and educates about transgender issues. She started Transgender Education and Awareness Month (TEAM) in November 2002 at the Gay and Lesbian Community Center of Utah (later renamed the Utah Pride Center). The events brought more visibility to transgender people and issues within the community. Storni is pictured here leading the Transgender March in the 2013 Pride Parade. (Courtesy David Daniels.)

The Bad Kids Collective began as a community of queer artists seeking positive change through art and self-expression. Founded by Cartel Chameleon, Lamia, Willard Cron, and Klaus von Austerlitz, the collective continues to grow in membership. Members combine elements of live music and drag, including gender queer aesthetics, during their performances to promote a message of self-empowerment and community engagement. (Courtesy Jesse Walker.)

The Matrons of Mayhem are camp drag queen performers, as seen by their colorful wigs and exaggerated costumes. Since the mid-2000s, they have hosted drag bingo on the third Friday of the month at First Baptist Church. The money raised is donated to a preselected local charity. They raised $3,875 for the Salt Lake Men's Choir, the highest amount to date. Pictured is Kirk Burkle reading numbers next to Petunia Pap Smear. (Courtesy Matrons of Mayhem.)

Erika Munson cofounded Mormons Building Bridges with Kendall Wilcox and Bianca Morrison Dillard in 2012 to foster ties between the LDS Church and the LGBT community. The group received wide media coverage when members marched for the first time in the 2012 Utah Pride Parade. Since then, local chapters have marched in other parades around the country. (Courtesy David Daniels.)

Attorneys Paul Burke (left) and Brett Tolman (center) filed an amicus brief in February 2013 for the Utah Pride Center asking the US Supreme Court (SCOTUS) to overturn the Defense of Marriage Act and California's Proposition 8. The then executive director of the Utah Pride Center, Valerie Larabee (right), held a SCOTUS watch party at the center, where the community learned about the rulings from the SCOTUS blog. (Courtesy David Daniels.)

Donna Weinholtz grew up in Florida before moving to Utah. She is the vice chair of Equality Utah and a well-known activist for and ally to the LGBT community. Her husband, Mike Weinholtz (right), ran for governor in 2016. They support a variety of organizations and events in Utah through the Weinholtz Family Foundation. (Courtesy David Daniels.)

US district judge Robert J. Shelby was born in Wisconsin. He served in the Utah Army National Guard from 1988 to 1996. He graduated from Utah State University in 1994 and the University of Virginia School of Law in 1998. President Obama nominated Shelby to the federal bench in 2011, and the US Senate confirmed him in 2012. Sen. Mike Lee (R-Utah) described Shelby as "preeminently qualified" for the position. Judge Shelby became the most talked about federal judge after he struck down Amendment 3 in 2013. He is pictured here speaking to a group of students at Utah State University. (Courtesy the *Herald Journal*.)

On December 20, 2013, author Seth Anderson (right) and Michael Ferguson became the first same-sex couple in Utah to marry. Paul Burke, a friend and attorney, called them when Shelby's ruling became available to say they could legally marry but that he did not know how much time they had to do so. Anderson and Ferguson rushed to the Salt Lake County Clerk's office expecting to find a line of people waiting to marry, but they were the only couple there. (Courtesy Jeff Anderson.)

As news of the ruling spread, hundreds of same-sex couples rushed to the county clerk's office to marry. Even though it was a holiday weekend, the office remained open later than usual to accommodate the historic decision. The room erupted in cheers each time a couple exited the office with a marriage license in hand. (Courtesy B. Jane Hudson.)

After the ruling and without a stay from the court, same-sex couples began to marry in Salt Lake City. Salt Lake City district attorney Sim Gill told the media that the legal ruling was clear and unambiguous and that "as of this moment, that is what the law of the land in the state of Utah is." (Courtesy David Daniels.)

After learning that Judge Shelby had struck down Amendment 3, on December 20, 2013, Penny Kirby (left) and Terri Henry went to the Utah County Clerk's Office, but Utah County clerk Bryan Thompson refused to issue a license. Instead, the office gave the women a letter explaining the county's reason for denying them their right to marry: the office was waiting for "further clarification from the state." They finally married on the morning of December 23, 2013, in Salt Lake City. (Courtesy Penny Kirby.)

An estimated 1,300 same-sex couples married in the weeks after Judge Shelby overturned Amendment 3, but Gov. Gary Herbert and Attorney General Sean Reyes vowed to fight the ruling. After the Supreme Court stayed the decision, Reyes said the state would not recognize the marriages performed as legal. On January 10, 2014, the community gathered at the capitol building for the Let It Stand rally to show solidarity and to demand that the state government honor and uphold the law. (Courtesy David Daniels.)

When the legislature refused to hear the seventh nondiscrimination bill in 2014, thirteen activists blocked the entrance to a legislative committee hearing and demanded it be heard. State senator Stuart Reid (R-Ogden) called the Utah Highway Patrol to arrest the activists on charges of disrupting a public meeting and disorderly conduct. Dubbed the "Capitol 13" in the press, they were sentenced to 90 days probation for the action. (Courtesy David Newkirk.)

Mark Lawrence (center), founder of the nonprofit Restore Our Humanity, assembled the team of six plaintiffs and hired the law firm that would challenge Utah's Amendment 3. Plaintiffs Kate Call (left) and her wife, Karen Archer, had legally married in Council Bluffs, Iowa, in 2011, but like others, their marriage was not recognized in Utah, which left them without protections afforded to married heterosexual couples. (Courtesy Jolene Mewing.)

The plaintiffs in *Kitchen v. Herbert* traveled to Denver, Colorado, for oral arguments at the US Court of Appeals for the Tenth Circuit on April 10, 2014. From left to right are Laurie Wood, Kodi Partridge, Derek Kitchen, Moudi Sbeity, Kate Call, and Karen Archer, pictured speaking to the press after the case had been argued before the judges. (Courtesy Jolene Mewing.)

The attorney for the plaintiffs, Peggy Tomsic (foreground, left) from the firm Magleby Cataxinos & Greenwood, spoke to reporters after oral arguments at the Tenth Circuit Court of Appeals in Denver, Colorado on April 10, 2014. In court, she argued that Amendment 3 violated the Fourteenth Amendment of the Constitution. Two months later, the Tenth Circuit affirmed 2-1 the decision of Judge Shelby but stayed its decision because it anticipated an appeal to the US Supreme Court. (Courtesy Jolene Mewing.)

Utah attorney general Sean Reyes spoke to the press after oral arguments. Phil Lott and Stan Purser, assistant attorneys general, argued for the state. On October 6, 2014, the United States Supreme Court denied review of not only Utah's appeal, but also six other petitions related to marriage equality, thus returning the right to marry to a majority of states. (Courtesy Jolene Mewing.)

After eight years, the legislature passed a nondiscrimination bill in 2015. Lauded in the press as "The Utah Compromise," the bill struck a balance between LGBT rights and religious freedom. The law bans employers and landlords from discriminating based on sexual orientation and gender identity while exempting religious organization and their affiliates from the law. Equality Utah executive director Troy Williams addressed the media at this press conference in the Governor's Reception Room at the Utah State Capitol. (Courtesy David Newkirk.)

Dr. Caitlyn Ryan has spent 40 years working with LGBT youth. In 2002, she began the Family Acceptance Project to help "ethnically, socially and religiously diverse families support their LGBT children." Her groundbreaking research shows through empirical evidence how parental and family reactions to their LGBT children contribute to the child's health and mental health development. She frequently speaks at conferences in Utah about her research and has received numerous awards. (Courtesy Mitch Mayne.)

The Evergreen Foundation presents. . .

YOU DON'T HAVE TO BE GAY

Developing A Healthy Male Identity

Friday, May 4, 1990
9:00 A.M. to 4:00 P.M.
Salt Lake City,Utah
at the
Marriott Hotel

In this conference, the first of its kind in the Mountain States, we will cover new and previously overlooked thinking about the origins of homosexuality, why it has taken so long to understand this dilemma, and how doors are now beginning to open. We will explore the stages of growth out of homosexuality into a healthy male identity. You already know what doesn't work. We will share all we know of what does work. You will have the opportunity to hear and talk with two leaders of the ex-gay movement and with counselors who work daily with men going through this process. They have seen long term development happen in many men with gratifying, and in some cases dramatic results. We will then focus on the new programs beginning along the Wasatch Front. Come join with us in learning about this controversial and exciting new work.

Can homosexuality be overcome?

"Yes it can!"

is our confident answer.

I used to think there was no hope of climbing out of homosexuality. I didn't even think I would be able to recognize a change if it did occur. I was wrong. Change and growth are attainable. I see myself and others through different eyes now. I have found friendship and peace.

—Tom G., Midvale, Utah

Like many other men who remain silent, I never in any way acted out on my homosexual feelings; hurting, celibate and alone. The world of my friends and family had long passed me by. I was going nowhere and tried everything to get out. Now I have found the path. I have fought my way far enough along it to know that I will become one of the very men that I once used to idolize.

—David T., Salt Lake City, Utah

When I was gay I lived in a glass prison with walls made of fear, anger, hate, and resentment. It took me years of effort to dissolve those walls. How much easier it would have been if this information had been available to me then.

—Janet E., Salt Lake City, Utah

With the guidance of the Lord and an insightful therapist, I learned how to overcome my childhood deficits and developed a more mature level of psychosexuality. Through this healing process I was able to overcome the homosexual addiction which held me in bondage for over 25 years.

—Gary K., Salt Lake City, Utah

For many years I believed I must have been born gay, having never experienced the least heterosexual interest. Nevertheless, I never became sexually involved with anyone. About 8 years ago, God revealed to me that I wasn't born gay by showing me its real cause. With this new insight I have gradually gotten free of the homosexual inclinations and I feel myself moving steadily toward full heterosexuality.

Utah has strong ties to the ex-gay movement, including a history of conversion therapy. Though not sponsored by the LDS Church, the Evergreen Foundation did have an affiliation. The group utilized LDS Church facilities, and prominent leaders of the church sat on the board of directors. This flier advertises an Evergreen conference and states emphatically, "Can homosexuality be overcome? Yes it can!" (Courtesy University of Utah.)

Evergreen International held its 19th annual conference in the Joseph Smith Memorial Building in 2009. Speakers included Dr. Joseph Nicolosi, one of the most prominent advocates for conversion therapy, and LDS general authority Bruce Hafen, who said being gay "is not in your DNA." Books for sale at the conference included titles such as *Overcoming Homosexuality: Developing Heterosexual Attraction* and *You Don't Have to Be Gay*. (Courtesy Michael Ferguson.)

Dr. John Dehlin and four other researchers published their study "Sexual Orientation Change Efforts among Current or Former LDS Church Members" in peer-reviewed academic journals, including the *Journal of Counseling Psychology*. With a sample size of 1,612 participants, the overall results of the study found that efforts to change from a homosexual to a heterosexual orientation are overwhelmingly reported to be either ineffective or damaging. (Courtesy TEDx Utah State University.)

Former Utah senator Scott McCoy (center) and Affirmation board member Sam Wolfe (right), both attorneys for the Southern Poverty Law Center, represented Utahn Michael Ferguson (left) and five others in *Ferguson v. JONAH*, a landmark case against conversion therapy in New Jersey. Defendants called two witnesses from the Utah-based North Star International to testify. After a three-week trial, the jury found the defendants liable for consumer fraud. For the first time in history, the court found that being gay is not a mental illness that can be cured. Coplaintiff Chaim Levin is shown reading the decision with Wolfe outside of the courthouse. (Courtesy Karsten Moran.)

Sophia Haws-Tingey, a Navy veteran and a software engineer, ran for Midvale City Council District 2 in 2015. The campaign made her the first transgender person in Utah to run in a general election. The Gay and Lesbian Victory Fund endorsed her campaign, and although she did not win the election, she received 42 percent of the vote. (Courtesy Victor Hugo Pinilla-Coxe.)

Jackie Biskupski returned to politics in 2015 when she ran for mayor of Salt Lake City. She defeated two-term incumbent Ralph Becker with 51.5 percent of the vote. She is the first openly LGBT mayor and second female mayor of Salt Lake City. Biskupski is pictured here being sworn in on January 4, 2016, next to her longtime partner and now wife, Betty Iverson. (Courtesy Stuart Graves.)

The University of Utah employs a variety of talented scholars working in the fields of gender and sexuality. Beth Clement is an associate professor of history and teaches courses on women's history, the history of sexuality, and the history of family. She is the director of the HIV/AIDS Oral History Project and oversaw the creation of the Kristen Ries & Maggie Snyder HIV/AIDS Archive at the Marriott Library. She has received the Virgil Award for Graduate Teaching and the Distinguished Teaching Award. (Courtesy B. Jane Hudson.)

Kathryn Stockton is a distinguished professor of English and associate vice president for equity and diversity at the University of Utah. She teaches queer theory, race theory, and the 19th-century novel and has authored several books, including *The Queer Child, or Growing Sideways in the Twentieth Century*, a finalist for the Lambda Literary Award in LGBT studies. In 2013, she received the Rosenblatt Prize for Excellence, the highest honor granted by the University of Utah. (Courtesy Kathryn Stockton.)

Lisa Diamond is a professor of psychology and gender studies at the University of Utah. Her research focuses on the development of sexual desire, identity, and orientation. She is best known for her groundbreaking research on female sexuality and the phenomenon of sexual fluidity that she published in her book *Sexual Fluidity: Understanding Women's Love and Desire.* (Courtesy Michael Ferguson.)

Stan Penfold, the first gay man elected to the Salt Lake City Council (in 2010), proposed renaming 900 South as Harvey Milk Boulevard in 2015. Other streets in the city are named after activists such as Martin Luther King Jr., Rosa Parks, and Cesar Chavez. The city council unanimously approved the proposal, and on May 14, 2016, a large block party celebrated the new name. (Courtesy Stan Penfold.)

Utah native Misty K. Snow won the Utah Democratic nomination for US Senate on June 28, 2016, making Snow one of two transgender candidates ever nominated by a major political party to run in a federal election. Her platform included raising the minimum wage to $15 per hour, paid maternity leave, LGBT equality, and cleaning Utah's air. She lost to Republican incumbent Mike Lee in the general election, but received 27 percent of the vote. (Courtesy Misty K. Snow for Senate Campaign.)

From humble beginnings with just a few dozen people in attendance, the Utah Pride festival has grown to become the second-largest civic event in the state. As more people came out to friends and family over the past 40 years, myths and fears about LGBT people began to shift towards inclusion, acceptance, and love. Although incredible progress has been made in Utah, the fight for full equality for LGBT citizens will continue. (Courtesy David Newkirk.)

Bibliography

Bringhurst, Newell G., and John C. Hamer, eds. *Scattering of the Saints: Schism within Mormonism*. Independence, MO: John Whitmer Books, 2007.

Canaday, Margot. *The Straight State: Sexuality and Citizenship in Twentieth Century America*. Princeton, NJ: Princeton University Press, 2011.

Chauncey, George. *Gay New York: Gender, Urban Culture and the Making of the Gay Male World 1890–1940*. New York: Basic Books, 1995.

D'Emilio, John. *Making Trouble: Essays on Gay History, Politics, and the University*. New York: Routledge, 1992.

Doyle, Vincent. *Making Out in the Mainstream: GLAAD and the Politics of Respectability*. Montreal: McGill-Queen's University Press, 2016.

Erzen, Tanya. *Straight to Jesus: Sexual and Christian Conversions in the Ex-Gay Movement*. Berkeley: University of California Press, 2006.

Faderman, Lillian. *The Gay Revolution: The Story of the Struggle*. New York: Simon & Schuster, 2015.

Foucault, Michel. *History of Sexuality, vol. 1: An Introduction*. New York: Vintage Books, 1978.

Gould, Deborah B. *Moving Politics: Emotion and ACT UP's Fight against AIDS*. Chicago: University of Chicago Press, 2009.

Jacobs, Sue-Ellen, Wesley Thomas, and Sabine Lang, eds. *Two-Spirit People: Native American Gender Identity, Sexuality, and Spirituality*. Urbana: University of Illinois Press, 1997.

Kristen Ries & C. Maggie Snyder HIV/AIDS Archive. Special Collections. J. Willard Marriott Library, University of Utah.

Newton, Esther. *Mother Camp: Female Impersonators in America*. Chicago: University of Chicago Press, 1972.

O'Donovan, Connell. *The Abominable & Detestable Crime Against Nature: A Revised History of Homosexuality & Mormonism, 1840–1980*. Salt Lake City: Signature Books, 1994.

Pearson, Carol Lynn. *Goodbye, I Love You: The True Story of a Wife, Her Homosexual Husband—and a Love Honored for Time and All Eternity*. New York: Random House, 1986.

Petro, Anthony M. *After the Wrath of God: AIDS, Sexuality, and American Religion*. New York: Oxford University Press, 2015.

Quinn, D. Michael. *Same Sex Dynamics Among Nineteenth Century Americans: A Mormon Example*. Champaign: University of Illinois Press, 1996.

Stein, Marc. *Rethinking the Gay and Lesbian Movement*. New York: Routledge, 2012.

Utah Pride Center Records, 1976–2001. Special Collections. J. Willard Marriott Library, University of Utah.

Waidzunas, Tom. *The Straight Line: How the Fringe Science of Ex-Gay Therapy Oriented Sexuality*. Minneapolis: University of Minnesota Press, 2015.

White, Heather R. *Reforming Sodom: Protestants and the Rise of Gay Rights*. Chapel Hill: University of North Carolina Press, 2015.

Williams, Walter L. *The Spirit and the Flesh: Sexual Diversity in American Indian Culture*. Boston: Beacon Press, 1986.

Winkler, Doug. "Lavender Sons of Zion: A History of Gay Men in Salt Lake City, 1950–1979" PhD diss., University of Utah, Salt Lake City, 2008.

Consistent with our mission to preserve history on a local level, this book was printed in South Carolina on American-made paper and manufactured entirely in the United States. Products carrying the accredited Forest Stewardship Council (FSC) label are printed on 100 percent FSC-certified paper.